AUTHENTIC
MINISTRY

Union

AUTHENTIC MINISTRY

SERVING FROM THE HEART

MICHAEL REEVES

Authentic Ministry: Serving from the Heart

Copyright © 2022 by Michael Reeves

www.UnionPublishing.org
Bridgend, United Kingdom

Unless otherwise noted, Scripture quotations are from The ESV® Bible (The Holy Bible, English Standard Version®), copyright © 2001 by Crossway, a publishing ministry of Good News Publishers. Used by permission. All rights reserved.

Cover and book design by Rubner Durais

ISBN 978-1-9168995-0-6 (paperback)
ISBN 978-1-9168995-2-0 (eBook)

For all the students
at Union School of Theology,
past and present.

Contents

Pay Careful Attention
to Yourselves

In Acts 20, Paul spoke to the elders of the church at Ephesus, charging them: "Pay careful attention to yourselves and to all the flock, in which the Holy Spirit has made you overseers, to care for the church of God, which he obtained with his own blood" (v. 28).

When thinking about Christian ministry, or preparing students for it, it is all too easy to think only about Paul's second command here: to pay attention to *the flock* and how we might best serve others. This is an easy shortcut, one that allows us to focus on growing our pastoral skills and our biblical knowledge, all the while leaving our own hearts unsearched. It leaves the door open to hypocrisy and hollow professionalism. It ushers in a horde of troubles, from burnout to bullying, from anxiety to isolation.

But Paul's second exhortation builds upon the foundation of the first: "Pay careful attention *to yourselves*." Only when we first do that can we have an authentic ministry that is able—from a position of health—to care rightly for all the flock of God. The simple aim of this little book is to help you pay attention to yourself and so cultivate the inner fitness necessary for outward service of the church.

The chapters that follow come from talks I have given to my students at Union School of Theology. These were not the theological lectures they would receive on topics like the trustworthiness of Scripture or the sufficiency of Christ, vital though those are. They were more like a *bon voyage* greeting, a "Godspeed!" to men and women starting out in their preparation for ministry. I gave them as a small part of an effort that they might not wear their learning like an impressive cloak to hide shriveled souls. I offer them to you now that you might serve with integrity, resilience, and joy.

1

Delight in God

One of the most beautiful, prize flowers of Reformation thought is the first question and answer of the Westminster Shorter Catechism, and it distills vast amounts of biblical thought into one gorgeous call and response. Here it is:

> *Question:* What is the chief end of man?
> *Answer:* Man's chief end is to glorify God, and to enjoy
> him forever.

The glory of God and enjoyment of him: these inseparable twin truths were guiding lights for the Reformation. The Reformers held that through all the doctrines they fought for and upheld, God was glorified, and people were given comfort and joy.

This was a guiding light for the Reformation, and it must be a guiding light for us who minister to others. What is our chief end in all we do? To glorify God, and to enjoy *him* in our ministry.

Delighting in God is what we were made for. Delighting in God is what we were saved for. Peter writes in 1 Peter 3:18 that "Christ also suffered once for sins, the righteous for the unrighteous, that he might *bring us to God*" (emphasis added). We are forgiven that we might be brought to know and find our joy in him; we are rescued from death not for some abstract life, but for the only true life of knowing him.

Then—and only then!—do we think and feel straight, when the one preeminent in reality becomes preeminent in our thoughts. He is the treasure and "very great" reward of the gospel (Gen. 15:1), and so our ministry must flow out of an enjoyment of him. It cannot move on from an enjoyment of him. If it does, it becomes dully hollow and hypocritical. That is, if you live and grow in your knowledge about God but do not grow in your delight in God, you are only hardening in sin and hypocrisy.

Indeed, this is the ultimate purpose of all theology: not merely to gather information, but to know, love, and enjoy God, the one who is the truth.

And yet this is something theology students and those training in theological colleges always struggle with. Jesus so easily becomes an object for me to dissect under a microscope. The gospel becomes a subject I master rather than a message I am mastered by. Scripture becomes a textbook I work with and plunder for essays and sermons rather than the active Word of the living God.

The Puritan Richard Baxter warned of this Christian professionalism—using Scripture and the knowledge of God simply to get the next essay done, or the next sermon done—with this painful analogy: "Many a tailor goes in rags, that maketh costly clothes for others; and many a cook scarcely licks his fingers, when he hath dressed for others the most costly dishes."[1] Walking this path, we become hollow people, neglecting communion with God, using the knowledge of God for some other end, for some job, not to know God. We *use* God instead of *enjoying* God.

And in that prayerless, praiseless place, our lives have turned ugly: cut off from real life, they have actually started to work against what we are made for: to glorify God and to enjoy him forever.

Sometimes we find ourselves tiring of Jesus, imagining that we have seen all there is to see and used up all the pleasure there is to be had in him. We get spiritually bored. But Jesus has satisfied the mind and heart of the infinite God

1 Richard Baxter, *The Reformed Pastor* (Edinburgh: Banner of Truth Trust, 1974), 54.

for eternity. Our boredom is simple blindness. If the Father can be infinitely and eternally satisfied in him, then he must be overwhelmingly all-sufficient for us—in every situation, for all eternity. And that's why the gospel is not lacking, because he is not lacking.

Now, let me just unpack this briefly, as we need to be thoroughly convinced if this is to make a difference. Our delight in God is so essential because it 1) distinguishes us from demons, 2) is the heartbeat of the saints, 3) is part of entering the true life of God, and 4) is what we were made for.

First, our delight in God distinguishes us from demons. James writes, "You believe that God is one; you do well. Even the demons believe—and shudder!" (2:19). Even the demons know their Bible and can explain it accurately. What distinguishes them from saints is not their knowledge: it is that where saints delight in God, demons dread him.

Jonathan Edwards once took it further:

> The devil once seemed to be religious from fear of torment. Luke 8:28, "When he saw Jesus, he cried out, and fell down before him, and with a loud voice said, 'What have I to do with thee, Jesus, thou Son of God most high? I beseech thee, torment me not.'" Here is external

worship. The devil is religious; he prays: he prays in a humble posture; he falls down before Christ, he lies prostrate; he prays earnestly, he cries with a loud voice; he uses humble expressions—"I beseech thee, torment me not"—he uses respectful, honorable, adoring expressions—"Jesus, thou Son of God most high." Nothing was wanting but love.[2]

Second, delight in God is the heartbeat of the new man, the spiritual nature. Saints love to cry out to their Father and echo David's desire in Psalm 27:4: "One thing have I asked of the LORD, that will I seek after: that I may dwell in the house of the LORD all the days of my life, to gaze upon the beauty of the LORD and to inquire in his temple."

Third, this delight in God we have is a core part of what it means to enter the true life of God. For eternity, God the Father has loved—delighted in—his perfect Son, and the Son has loved and delighted in his Father in the fellowship of the Spirit. We have been created that we might share that (cf. John 17:20–23).

And lastly, as we have already been reminded by the Westminster Catechism, delight in God is what we were

---

2 Jonathan Edwards, *Works of Jonathan Edwards*, ed. Sang Hyun Lee, vol. 21, *Writings on the Trinity, Faith, and Grace* (New Haven: Yale University Press, 2003), 171.

made for. It is crucial to Christian life, service, fruitfulness, and happiness. Here's how John Calvin put it:

> It will not suffice simply to hold that there is One whom all ought to honor and adore, unless we are also persuaded that he is the fountain of every good, and that we must seek nothing elsewhere than in him. ... For until men recognize that they owe everything to God, that they are nourished by his fatherly care, that he is the Author of their every good, that they should seek nothing beyond him—they will never yield him willing service. Nay, unless they establish their complete happiness in him, they will never give themselves truly and sincerely to him.[3]

Delighting in God is therefore the root and happy secret behind growing in Christ, serving the church, and blessing the world. It is not something extra that we add on to a list of righteous actions but the very ground and source of righteous living. So, friends, keep making sure of this: that all your ministry and all your life is an act of

---

3 John Calvin, *Institutes of the Christian Religion*, ed. John T. McNeill, trans. Ford Lewis Battles (Philadelphia: Westminster Press, 1960), 1.2.1.

worship—full of prayer, full of praise, which are fuel for your enjoyment of God.

And for those who are studying for the ministry, this will make your studies that much more enjoyable. As one theologian put it,

> The theologian who has no joy in his work is not a theologian at all. Sulky faces, morose thoughts, and boring ways of speaking are intolerable in this science. May God deliver us from what the Catholic Church reckons one of the seven sins of the monk—*taedium* [weariness]—in respect of the great spiritual truths with which theology has to do. But we must know, of course, that it is only God who can keep us from it.[4]

We were made to enjoy "the light of the knowledge of the glory of God in the face of Jesus Christ" (2 Cor. 4:6). That is the only light in which we can have life. It is the only light in which we can have full hearts. It is the only light in which we can minister to others.

---

4 Karl Barth, *Church Dogmatics*, ed. G. W. Bromiley and T. F. Torrance, trans. T. H. L. Parker et al., vol. 2, pt. 1, *The Doctrine of God* (Edinburgh: T&T Clark, 1957), 656.

If you try to minister without constantly re-filling your eyes and heart with this light, then in the power of your own adrenaline and wisdom you will go out and you will burn out. But fill your eyes with the glory of Christ; ensure that he is glorious to you—and then, of course, you will not want to proclaim yourself. In his light you see that he is glorious, and you are not. When he is glorious to you, out of a full heart you will want to share him. This is the essence of authentic ministry.

The glory of God in the face of Jesus Christ is the only light that can overcome darkness. Hold your gaze on nothing less. Settle for nothing less. Herald nothing less.

2

Boast Only in the Cross

"But far be it from me to boast except in the cross of our Lord Jesus Christ, by which the world has been crucified to me, and I to the world." – Galatians 6:14

The seed of all sickness in the Christian life is the failure to boast in the cross. The seed of all health is boasting in the cross. Yet how easy it is to think we can move on from such basics of the gospel.

"I boast only in the cross." This is an astonishing statement from Paul, for he had so much else he could have boasted in: he was a Hebrew of Hebrews, a Pharisee (Phil. 3:5). So learned, so intelligent, such authority—he was given special visions and revelations. And he was an apostle! But his boast is the cross.

And hear Paul very clearly: he is not simply saying that he wants to be a person who merely talks about the cross. This is not a call just to say the right, Christian things. Anyone can do that. Paul is speaking of boasting. It is a heart issue: his concern is with what delights him, what captivates him.

What mattered to Paul—what matters to God—is not circumcision or uncircumcision, but a new creation (Gal. 6:15). By "new creation" he means a new heart, with new loves and new desires. What matters is not what's on the outside—our badges of religion. What matters is a heart that is enthralled with the cross of Jesus Christ.

The cross is the pinnacle of Christ's work and the clearest window into his identity. It is the fulcrum of the gospel and the magnet that draws people to God. Stirring oratory, soaring music, learned philosophy, and clever arguments: none have the power to stir the deep affections of human hearts like a faithful exhibition of Jesus crucified.

Before we are confronted by the cross, we blithely suppose ourselves to be rather nice and pleasant, or, at the very least, we suppose that we deserve to be in the right with God and men. What awareness we have of our faults is superficial and excused. But through the sight of the cross, God humbles us by sharing with us his own disgust at sin, letting us feel the justice of his sentence of death upon us. We find ourselves shocked and horrified at what we are.

That all sounds odious to a culture of self-esteem, but it is work of real divine kindness. All my natural avoidance of guilt—all the blame-shifting and excuses—is ended under the shadow of the cross, and it is ended so that the guilt can be faced and resolved.

The cross is the message that brings the dead to life, and the message that enlivens *all*—the spiritually sluggish as well. Christians who want to grow in holiness and Christians who have grown apathetic; unbelievers and those unsure about their spiritual state: *all* find change of heart at the cross. That is why the gospel we proclaim to our people, to the world—and, most of all, to ourselves—must be a cross-shaped and cross-centered gospel.

The human heart is incapable of reforming itself, and yet in our natural self-dependence we think that mere determination can bring about the deep self-improvement we crave. At such times we rake our performance and our hearts in the hope that we might feel secure in them. But it is only at the foot of the cross, where our sin and God's judgment and grace are supremely revealed, that we will find a true change of heart.

Why is it that the message of Jesus' death is so uniquely powerful to enlighten the blind, awaken the dead, and enliven the sluggish Christian? Quite simply, it is because in the cross of Christ we see most clearly the glory of God. "For God, who said, 'Let light shine out of darkness,' has shone in our hearts to give the light of the knowledge of the glory of God in the face of Jesus Christ" (2 Cor. 4:6). It is the glory of God which shines light into otherwise impenetrable darkness, and it is by beholding the glory of the Lord that anyone is transformed "from one degree of glory to another" (2 Cor. 3:18).

At the cross, the true wisdom, power, holiness, goodness, love, and sovereignty of God are revealed in all their surprising beauty, winning the hearts of those who look to him. And while God is *always* wise, powerful, holy, good, loving, and sovereign, we do not understand or see that aright apart from Christ. His sovereignty, for example, we would mistake for cold tyranny or unfeeling government; his goodness we would take for weak indulgence.

When the glory of God is displayed in the cross, we get to see *all* God's perfections. We see that God is not merely helpful to the weak, but long-suffering and infinitely merciful to great sinners. We see the riches of his grace, his sovereign power to save, his holy justice, and his love. His bleeding makes our hearts bleed, and his shame makes us ashamed. In the cross we see a divine disgust at sin that makes sin appalling in our eyes too.

But more: through the cross we see a love so fierce it pierces our apathy and overwhelms desire for other things. At the cross we see the majestic goodness of Christ and the sweet security we can have in him. That is why it can transform the vicious, the sad, the despairing, and the selfish into joy-filled, radiantly generous, and kind saints.

The cross is also where we receive a new identity.

Paul writes that at the cross, "the world has been crucified to me, and I to the world." All who throw themselves on Jesus find their achievements are no longer the true ground of their identity. With all my sin and failings, I have been crucified with Christ. And now *he* is my identity.

Yet today, everywhere I turn, I see Christians struggling precisely because of a failure to find their identity in Christ.

For me, I find the weight of what I do with my time, the sheer allotment of my hours, makes me think I *am* what I do. And thus, ever so quietly, I come to think of myself primarily, not as crucified with Christ, but as successful or unsuccessful, popular or unpopular—depending on how the day is going. Bluntly, when not defined by Christ, I find myself as fragile as a puffed-up balloon.

When I begin to define myself by success or popularity, they matter far too much to me: if I get them, my ego inflates preposterously; if I don't, I implode. That simply cannot happen when the core of my identity is consciously found in Christ, for he is the same, yesterday, today, and forever (Heb. 13:8).

The source of our identity affects more than just our own personal sanity: when Christians define themselves by something other than Christ, they poison the air all round. When they crave power and popularity and they get it, they become pompous, patronizing, or simply bullies. And when they don't get it, they become bitter, apathetic, or prickly. Whether flushed by success or burnt by lack of it, both have cared too much for the wrong thing. Defining themselves by something other than Christ, they become something other than Christ: ugly.

This truth has deep plough-work to do in our hearts. When we first trusted in Christ, we were immediately given a new status, but for that status to be felt as the deepest truth about ourselves is radical, ongoing business. Our status in Christ is the primary identity of the believer, though, and the only foundation for truly Christian living. For our health, our joy, and our fellowship, then, we must take up arms against the insidious idea that we have any identity—any background, ability, or status—more basic or more essential than that of being crucified with Christ and sharing the Son's own life together before the Father.

Much else has been written about the trials of Christian leadership, but finding your identity in the wrong place is perhaps one of the most common and invisible traps for the Christian leader.

Let's consider the leader who forgets that he is a sinner saved by grace and not his own efforts, the leader who finds his identity not in Christ but in his pastoring: how will his ministry play out? If he slips into thinking he is justified by his works—and the most orthodox Christian can make this error—he will be driven by his works. If he forgets he is a sinner saved by grace, he may try to fake his own perfection in front of his people. This is surprisingly common! If he forgets the cross and his justification before God and seeks to find his worth instead in the approval of others, he will never lead, but will merely pander to whatever makes him popular.

In other words, for the leader to have strength of purpose, integrity, and the ability not to be driven (and burned out) by his ministry, he must maintain a solid grasp on the cross and so on his justification.

No wonder Paul would only boast in the cross: what other boast offers joy and liberation? When the world is crucified to me, I am free from it. Then, the world has nothing like the cross to attract me. Money, career—the things of the world—are not what give me my joy and satisfaction. Christ is.

Times of reformation and renewal in the church have always been marked by this cross-centered perspective. A fresh sight of the glory and grace of God awakens people both to who he is and to who they are. Unlike what they once thought, they realize that he is great, glorious, and beautiful in his holiness—and they are not. At the lifting up of Christ on the cross, they are like Isaiah, whose vision of the Lord in glory, high and lifted up, caused him to cry, "Woe to me! … I am ruined! For I am a man of unclean lips, and I live among a people of unclean lips, and my eyes have seen the King, the LORD Almighty" (Isa. 6:5). Alternative gospels, where sin is a small problem and so Christ a small Savior, a mere assistant, never have the same effect.

The humility we learn at the foot of the cross, glorying in Christ and not ourselves, is the wellspring of all spiritual health. When our eyes are opened to the love of God for us sinners, we let slip our masks. Condemned as sinners yet justified in Christ, we can begin to be honest about ourselves. Loved despite all our unloveliness, we begin to love. Given peace with God, we begin to know an inner peace and joy. Shown the magnificence of God above all things, we become more resilient, trembling in wonder at God and not man.

This was the transformation Martin Luther experienced through the gospel. Luther often described himself as an anxious young man, so wrapped up in himself that every little thing frightened him. Even the sound of a leaf blown in the wind could make him flee (Lev. 26:36). That changed through his encounter with the gospel of Christ, as Roland Bainton recounts in the splendid final words of his biography:

> No longer did Luther tremble at the rustling of a wind-blown leaf, and instead of calling upon St. Anne he declared himself able to laugh at thunder and jagged bolts from out of the storm. This was what enabled him to utter such words as these: "Here I stand. I cannot do otherwise. God help me. Amen."[1]

The humility Luther found before the majesty and mercy of God was not gloomy or timid. It was full of joy and courage.

---

1 Roland H. Bainton, *Here I Stand: A Life of Martin Luther* (New York and Nashville: Abingdon, 1950), 386.

That is the hallmark of the humility that is found at the cross. It is the manner of one refreshed by the gospel.

When captivated by the magnificence of God, we will not be so drawn to human-centered therapeutic religion. Under the radiance of his glory, we will not want to establish our own little empires. Our tiny achievements will seem petty, our feuds and personal agendas odious. He will loom large, making us bold to please God and not men. We will not dither or stammer with the gospel. Instead, aware of our own redemption, we will share his own meekness and gentleness, not breaking a bruised reed (Isa. 42:3; Matt. 12:20). We will be quick to serve, quick to bless, quick to repent, and quick to laugh at ourselves, for our glory is not ourselves, but Christ. This is the integrity found through the lifting up of Christ on his cross.

Boasting in the cross is what we will do for eternity. It is what makes Christians *look* heavenly: humbled, liberated, rejoicing—gasping at God's kindness and mercy. It is the need of our day: men and women for whom Christ in his crucified glory eclipses all other dreams, hopes, and purposes; men and women who find Christ more satisfying than everything.

3

Pray Boldly

"Our Father in heaven" – Matthew 6:9

In Matthew 6:9, Jesus says: "Pray … like this, 'Our Father in heaven.'" These words open the floodgates of prayer—and heavenly blessing.

It could not be more important to look at prayer today, for we live in a world where people believe they are self-sufficient. They don't need to cry out for help. And Christians are swept along: we are becoming like busy Martha, doing our many tasks but failing to sit with Mary at Jesus' feet. But without prayer, Christians are hollow. For prayer is the mark of Christian integrity.

What is prayer? The answer to this question may seem obvious, but I think confusion over this is a real cause of much of our difficulty. Too many Christians think and speak about prayer as if it's just "one of those things Christians do."

It's yet another Christian activity, another item to check off the list. But you can think that you're praying when actually you're doing it all wrong. For example, the Lord says of Israel in Isaiah 29:13: "This people draw near with their mouth and honor me with their lips, while their hearts are far from me."

So, what is real prayer? John Calvin put it brilliantly. He said that prayer is "the chief exercise of faith."[1] In other words, prayer is the first and main way true faith expresses itself. For in true prayer, we actually depend upon God, and trust him. That is exercising faith. In prayer we show how much we *really* want communion with God, how much we *really* depend on him.

Prayerlessness is practical atheism.

If it is true that prayer is "the chief exercise of faith," then of course everything—the world, the flesh, and the devil—conspires against prayer. What does this mean? It means, my friend, that you're not the odd one out in your struggle with prayer. It is not *your* secret shame, and yours alone—which can be the crippling fear. You are just a sinner, naturally inclined away from faith and prayer. And you know who is the friend of sinners!

---

1 Calvin, *Institutes* 3.20.

So, if prayer is the chief exercise of faith, what is going to help us sinners pray? What is going to increase our faith? Paul tells us in Romans 10:17: faith comes by hearing the Word of God. Faith—and so prayer—is birthed by the gospel.

That's why Scripture and prayer are so often put together—why Daniel was encouraged to pray by reading Jeremiah (see 9:2). It is the Word of God, the gracious message of Christ, that awakens faith and so prayer. That, therefore, must be the basic shape of our everyday communion with God: we set Christ before ourselves. We hear the word of Christ in Scripture, in song, through each other, reminding ourselves as we praise him; we cry that our eyes might be opened to see the beauty of the Lord, that we might be drawn afresh to want him—and then prayer is just voicing our heart's response.

We breathe in Scripture, and we breathe out prayer. Breathe in, breathe out: that's the Christian life. Prayer is the breath of heavenly life: where that life is, there must be some prayer; where that life flourishes, there will be *much* prayer, and much *pleasure* in prayer. And friends, let us be clear: the life-breath of Christianity, of healthy churches, is not our talent, or even our hard work. It is prayer: active dependence upon God.

So, let's go to the Word of God, which feeds prayer. Jesus says, "Pray … like this: 'Our *Father* in heaven.'" The first thing Jesus would have pray-ers know is the name "Father." That's the first and most basic lesson in prayer.

Do you know God as your Father? If you have put your trust in Christ, he is! But often we tend to think of God as aloof in heaven: a distant ruler, too great to be interrupted by us sinners. He feels remote and we feel guilty, and so we don't dare go to him in prayer. Oh no, brothers and sisters: God is so great he cannot overlook you!

And the gospel means he is not a distant Lord in heaven: he has sent his Son to bring us back to himself that we might be adopted. That the Son might be firstborn among many brothers and sisters. That we might be his children, and that we might call him "Abba, Father!"

The theologian Jim Packer once wrote: "If you want to judge how well a person understands Christianity, find out how much he makes of the thought of being God's child, and having God as his Father. If this is not the thought that prompts and controls his worship and prayers and his whole outlook on life, it means that he does not understand Christianity very well at all."[2]

---

2 J. I. Packer, *Knowing God* (London: Hodder & Stoughton, 1973), 224.

Packer was right, for to call God "Father" *and mean it* is to understand the gospel well. Doing so means you understand that the Son, who has been eternally "in the lap of the Father" (John 1:18, my translation) has come to bring us that we might be with him there, that we who have rejected him might be brought back—and brought back not merely as creatures, but as children, to enjoy the abounding love the Son has always known.

Paul in his letters writes that "God has sent the Spirit of his Son into our hearts, crying 'Abba! Father!'" (Gal. 4:6; cf. Rom. 8:15). And have you noticed what a strange word he uses there? Paul writes all his letters in Greek, but here he has inserted this one Aramaic word, "Abba." Why? Why this word in a different language all of a sudden?

There is another place in Scripture where this term appears. If you turn to the scene in Mark 14 where Jesus is praying in the garden the night before he is killed, there you hear him talking in private to his Father and saying "Abba, Father" (v. 36). Paul is showing us as personally as he can that "sonship" means being given the very relationship with the Father that the Son himself has. We come before the Father now, just as Jesus always has. Just as Jesus does!

"Abba": this is Jesus' personal name for his Father, and he shares it with us. It is an intimate word. That's what Jesus shares with us: a child-like intimacy, trust, and love.

Knowing I am a beloved child of God protects me from thinking of prayer as a ladder to God, an exercise by which I work my way into his favor. No, prayer doesn't make me more accepted. Prayer is growing in the appreciation of what I have already been given. United to Christ, in him, I am a cherished son—and my Father delights to hear me. And to our Father, prayer is as incense. It is a pleasing smell to him. In other words, he delights to hear and help.

John Calvin said that we pray, as it were, through Jesus' mouth. The Father has always longed to hear the prayers of his dear Son—and we pray in his name. The Son gives us his name to pray in, so that we pray as him. That relationship between the Father and the Son is what we have been brought in to enjoy, and in prayer that is what we do. And so, once again, prayer is exercising faith: believing his almost incredible promise that I can come to him, sinful as I am. I believe the Most High is my loving Father.

Friends, the devil loves to fight us here. He will whisper, "You can't pray! Why would a holy God listen to such a sinner as you?" Don't listen. Don't think you need to prepare yourself before you can pray. If you feel too sinful to pray, or too spiritually cold, cry out to him for mercy. Call to the throne of grace. Your words will surely go into the loving ears of your Father.

And if still you feel you can't pray, look to the cross. The cross is God's guarantee that he will hear the prayers of his children. So, look to the blood of Christ when you pray. See how he has covered your sins. See how he has opened the way to heaven. See how he loves you. Can you doubt that he longs to hear from you?

Go to your Father: he promises he will hear and answer.

Let us now look at the next word Jesus uses to help us pray. He says, "Pray … like this: 'Our Father in *heaven*.'" This kind Father of ours is the heavenly King of all creation, the Lord of hosts.

At Union School of Theology, we have a Ph.D. program to raise up Christian leaders, and we offer this in partnership with the Free University of Amsterdam. The Free University of Amsterdam was founded by the great Calvinist theologian Abraham Kuyper, who in the early years of the twentieth century was also Prime Minister of the Netherlands. In his inaugural lecture for the University, Kuyper famously said, "There is not a square inch in the whole domain of our human existence over which Christ, who is Sovereign over *all*, does not cry: 'Mine!'"

Indeed, every molecule in the universe moves at God's command. There is no power, no authority, outside his control. He is not worried by a pandemic or a crisis: he has it on a chain, and he uses it for his glory. So when you come to him in prayer, come boldly to your Father, and come confidently, for he reigns over all.

In a hymn entitled "Encouragement to Pray," John Newton put it like this:

> You are coming to a King–
> Large petitions with you bring.
> For his grace and pow'r are such,
> None can ever ask too much.[3]

I never knew John Newton, of course, but I had the privilege of ministering together—and writing a book—with the pastor-theologian John Stott. Stott said he once visited a small village church when he was on holiday. Here is what he observed:

> When we came to the pastoral prayer, it was led by a
> lay brother, because the pastor was on holiday. So he

---

3 John Newton, "Encouragement to Pray," in *Trinity Psalter Hymnal* (Atlanta: Great Commission Publications, 2018), #789.

prayed that the pastor might have a good holiday. Well, that's fine. Pastors should have good holidays. Second, he prayed for a lady member of the church who was about to give birth to a child that she might have a safe delivery, which is fine. Third, he prayed for another lady who was sick, and then it was over. That's all there was. It took twenty seconds. I said to myself, it's a village church with a village God.[4]

Now, friends, the church has often been known for its fearless faith, for its bold praying in the face of impossible odds. And the Lord has blessed his people for it. And so I beg you now: do not lose that. Do not settle for small prayers to a small god. Do not be anxious like the world, running and hiding from problems like everyone else. For our Father is not a village god.

Don't pray cautious prayers for little things that you can see to yourself. You are coming to a King: large petitions with you bring. The greater your view of God, the more you will expect from him. And the more you expect from God, the more you are likely to receive.

---

4 John Stott, *Ten Great Preachers: Messages and Interviews*, ed. Bill Turpie (Grand Rapids: Baker, 2000), 117.

When you pray, don't think about the act of praying. Focus on the one you are praying to. Remember who you are coming before—for when your eyes go up and see the awesome sovereignty of our Father in heaven, your prayers will get bigger. He is not a village god.

But there's another important word Jesus uses when he teaches us "Pray like this, 'Our Father in heaven.'" He is *our* Father in heaven. Not just my Father, but *our* Father.

Have you ever wondered at that time recorded in Matthew 9, from verse 36? We read there: "When [Jesus] saw the crowds, he had compassion for them, because they were harassed and helpless, like sheep without a shepherd. Then he said to his disciples, 'The harvest is plentiful, but the laborers are few; therefore pray earnestly to the Lord of the harvest to send out laborers into his harvest'" (vv. 36–38).

Now, why did Jesus ask his disciples to pray this? Surely he could pray that. And wouldn't one prayer of his be more effective than all of theirs? But he wants them to join in with him, to share his concerns, to share his prayers, his mission.

And that's what we're doing in prayer: we are joining in the Son's fellowship with his Father, joining in his mission to the world. We pray with him, "Our Father." And what confidence that gives!

And we pray *our* Father because he brings us *together* to him as the Father's *family*. When we pray together, it is a little bit of heaven on earth, of gathering around the throne. This is true no matter when or where we come together in one spirit to kneel together before our one Father.

Then, our prayers for each other build up our love for each other. We feel our family fellowship together more. Then, we express what Jesus died to gain: we are a worldwide family, united by the blood of Jesus, sharing one Spirit, with our eyes all fixed on that same, sovereign throne of grace.

My beloved brothers and sisters, as you pray, you show how different we are to all the world. We are not an anxious people without help. We are not left to ourselves, having to protect and bless ourselves. We are not alone in the world, throwing up desperate prayers to a distant god who may or may not hear us. With boldness and with joy we get on our knees. And with fearless faith we pray, "Our Father in heaven."

God's Fatherly heart is near to all who call on him. And this same Fatherly heart wields the scepter that rules the world.

4

Relish Humility

"Do nothing from selfish ambition or conceit, but in humility count others more significant than yourselves."
– Philippians 2:3

A t the heart of true Christian integrity is humility.
That might sound hollow and even ridiculous given all the pride and power-politics that has sullied the name of Christianity in recent years. And it is not just the high-profile scandals. We evangelicals are people of the Word: learning is what we do. Yet learning so easily promotes arrogance. Then there is our conviction that we have the truth, an attitude that easily collapses into the sort of pharisaical fault-finding that makes many run and seek refuge elsewhere.

John Stott maintained that "the supreme quality which the evangelical faith engenders (or should do) is humility."

And yet, he admitted, "evangelical people are often regarded as proud, vain, arrogant and cocksure."[1]

What effect should the gospel have on us, though? "He must increase, but I must decrease" (John 3:30). For in the gospel is revealed the glory of the living, triune God, and in his light we creatures and sinners are exposed for the petty wretches we are.

In Philippians 2:1–13, we get to see the secret of humility and the heart of true ministry and leadership.

See, first of all, what Paul is doing here: he holds out Christ to us that we might adore him. That's very clear in Paul's wording, in how he couches this description of Christ: he means to affect his readers. You are supposed to read this description of the great Prince of Heaven who humbles himself to the cross for us with the result that you might willingly bend the knee, that you might have this mind that was in him.

That's what I call good theology! And that's the whole point of authentic Christian ministry. It is our joy to devote ourselves to learning, but as we fill our brains with the knowledge of Christ held out to us in Scripture, we do not seek simply to learn for the sake of learning; instead, we fill

---

1 John Stott, *Evangelical Truth: A Personal Plea for Unity* (Leicester: InterVarsity, 1999), 147.

our minds with the vision of Christ so that we might bow before him in adoration.

There's a tiny little book I'd thoroughly recommend to you, by Helmut Thielicke, called *A Little Exercise for Young Theologians*. And in it, Thielicke says that young students of theology are prone to go through a rather nasty stage he calls "theological puberty." It's the stage when, after a bit of study, you find yourself knowing more theology and Bible than any of your friends and family. Your knowledge outstrips anyone in a Bible study group, and you feel this rush of theological adrenaline.

There is a wonderful word sometimes used to describe students in their second year of study. They are called "sophomores." The word comes from two Greek words stitched together: σοφός (sophos), meaning "wise," and μωρός (moros), meaning "foolish." Sophomores are "wise fools." With a year's study under their belts they feel like theological geniuses, more knowledgeable and intelligent than anyone else. But their little knowledge has misled them and puffed them up. They are not yet truly wise, as they presume, but still harbor foolishness.

If you detect that tendency to self-congratulation in yourself, be very careful, for that pride is the polar opposite of what characterizes Christ here in Philippians. He, the one with supreme power, does not grasp, but rather pours himself out for the blessing of others. That is how Christ defines the nature of authentic ministry. It means you cannot serve Christ truly in an un-Christlike way.

The Puritans liked to talk about the "tincture" or atmosphere around a minister. This was a wise concern for a quality easily missed. They saw that it is not just the minister's abilities and competence that define his ministry. His *character* creates a particular atmosphere around him that people can detect, even if they can't quite put their finger on it. His kindness, his pride, his patience, his irritability: each gives off a particular aroma that can set the tone of his church quite as much as his teaching.

Of all those qualities, pride is especially malignant. Those of us who are called to theological pursuits may rightly crave theological strength. But the *source* of that strength makes a difference. A man strong *in himself* can very rarely proclaim a suffering Savior. His strength means he can't acknowledge the depth of Christ's mercy to him. His brilliance gets in the way of Christ's.

The first work of grace in the sinner is a pulling down of the old man and a demolition of his vaunting and deluded self-confidence and self-love. All our natural avoidance of guilt—all the blame-shifting and excuses, all the "mistakes were made, but not by me"—is ended. We are driven out of ourselves that we might trust only in Christ and not on ourselves anymore.

It is the stripping that allows us to be clothed with real beauty and righteousness. It is the enlightenment that makes us see our need for cleansing.

The knowledge of Christ is given to us not simply to slosh around in our heads—and certainly not to puff us up—but to transform our heart and character. The ultimate end of all our knowing is that we might love him and become more like him.

If you ignore this, and during your study pay mere lip service to the importance of your own growth in Christlikeness—if you effectively use your education simply to become more dominant, more impressive—it would probably be best if you stopped studying instead. For you will be modeling to the world a pride that at root is satanic, not the way of Christ.

And that brings us on to the second thing we see here: Paul gives us this description of Christ in order to transform us. Specifically, he wants us to share Christ's humility (2:5). This exhortation is for every Christian, but it is especially pertinent for those who are given power, for those who get exalted.

And within the church, it is often those with theological training who get exalted. Whatever it is you're going to do when you finish your studies or gain more theological knowledge, almost certainly you will be given more power, more authority—people will seek to put you on a pedestal.

Will you let them?

Success is hugely seductive. If you pursue success, you can usually make a name for yourself if you try hard enough, if you grasp for it and put yourself forward. But the story of the church is tragically littered with cautionary tales of fantastically gifted leaders who have crashed because of their lack of character. These are leaders who *started out* with a blazing heart and love for Christ and who were therefore given opportunity, given praise, given power. But eventually, it was proven that they didn't have the character to handle it.

If you are deepening in your knowledge of the Scriptures and Christian history and doctrine, then you can reasonably expect to be given opportunities and power and praise. The question is not "Will this happen?" The question is, when it does happen, will you have developed the Christlike servant-heartedness to handle however much you are given? And the more you are given, the more humility you will need, if you are not to become a power-abuser, if you are not to fall.

The more gifted you are, the more power and talent you have, the more good you may find you can do in the world—but also, the more harm you can do. And the path that you will follow depends upon whose mind you have. Will you follow your own mind? Or do you have the mind of Christ Jesus, who did not grasp his rightful equality with God, but emptied himself? Great good or great harm depends on this. Especially if you recognize yourself as naturally ambitious, put pride to death before disaster happens, whether that be slow and subtle or swift and catastrophic.

Tragically, I have to tell you that pride and the abuses of power that flow from it are everywhere in the leadership of the church today: self-service, power games, manipulation. And the damage done to Christ's people by un-Christlike leaders is incalculable.

This may seem obvious from where you sit. All of us have lamented the precipitous and public falls of once-respected church leaders. But the actions and attitudes that precede those falls are not as easily detectable. It's sometimes easy when you're young and you don't yet have that power to critique overbearing, pompous, or dictatorial leaders. But what we see on the surface isn't the root of the problem: a deeper trajectory gets set over years. The rot sets in before anyone can see it. And the same thing can happen within each of us.

So, fix your eyes on Christ, our beautiful and definitive leader. See how attractive is his humility, and resolve now, friends, to be humble, Christlike leaders. Let love for his humble generosity be your sword against your pride. Pride leads us to use other people, causing significant damage to lives and dishonoring the name of Christ across the world.

Don't mishear me: I'm not saying you should run away from power and opportunity for fear of how you might abuse it. No, work, learn, become theologically accomplished, and push with all your might to make Christ known. Seize the opportunities you're given: but watch very carefully for what will be a subtle, subtle shift into working for your own glory.

At this point you may stop and wonder: But isn't the bride of Christ, his church, supposed to have a grand vision of reformation? How does humility fit in with a healthy desire to make the name of Christ known?

This is exactly the point. It is *Christ* whom we are to make much of. Our focus must not be on what people think of us—their comments, critiques, or opinions—but on what God does. Surely we are to listen to those around us and to consider their point of view. Shepherds of the flock know their flocks intimately. But our boasting comes not in what others recognize that we have achieved, but in the cross.

The hinge of Philippians 2 is verse 5. But verses 3 and 4 provide the context that orient us: "Do nothing from self-ish ambition or conceit, but in humility count others more significant than yourselves. Let each of you look not only to his own interests, but also to the interests of others."

Paul states here his concern not just for individual hearts, but for the body of Christ. And this is a two-way street. First, if you don't have Christ's servant-mentality, then instead of looking to the interests of others, you will look only to your own. This breeds a detrimental culture of one-upmanship and rivalry. And here theological students need to watch for the dangers of the essay-marking system. Marking work is supposed to help you assess how you're doing, to encourage striving towards excellence—good and important aims. But in our sin we can use it to foster unhealthy competition between us, or simply to build a foundation for pride.

Don't go there! Seek to do excellently, but not to *out-do* brothers and sisters. No, let's develop together a culture of looking to the interests of others. Let's fight together to have a warm fellowship characterized by caring for each other through thick and through thin—a band of brothers and sisters who will then stick together in the struggles that come, for the glory of Christ. If we do that, imagine the wider fellowship that will ripple outward and strengthen the leadership of the churches in the generation to come.

And the other side to this matter of community is this: pride spoils community, but community can also help quell pride. We can support one another in this. One of the best things I took away from my time at college was a pair of friendships. These two friends and I still meet up three times a year and ask each other how we're doing spiritually. These conversations have been a lifeline, an oasis. I would love to see every one of you find such friends. Cultivate warm friendships while you study; have others around you who love you enough to tell you when they see your heart turning.

We've seen that Paul calls us to share Christ's humility (vv. 5–11) and that, together, we can help one another in that (vv. 3–4). Let's consider now the edges of the passage, which address the question of "how": How does Paul think we can change? How do we exchange our natural, lethal pride and selfish ambition for a heart that is Christlike?

Paul starts verse 1 like this: "So if there is any encouragement in Christ, any comfort from love, any participation in the Spirit[, then...]" Do you see what he is teaching here? Personal transformation begins and ends with the knowledge of Christ—it arises from the comfort and encouragement of knowing him. We don't naturally have the ability to pick ourselves up and make ourselves like Christ. It's when the Spirit opens our eyes to appreciate Christ that we want to be like him, for we see how his loving humility is so much more beautiful than our petty self-service.

To know Christ is to delight in him. So where do you find true delight? If you delight in yourself, you substitute what is false for what is true. Delighting in self is a form of self-deception. But when we delight in God, pride falls away as we fall at his feet.

That's why Paul describes Christ as he does, and that's his encouragement to us about how to change: look to Christ! See how much more satisfying he is and how marvelous are his ways, and you will be weaned off pride. In verse 12, Paul calls this "working out" your salvation.

This happens in a lesser way when you meet a truly humble, Christlike older Christian leader. Isn't that a moving experience? You can't help but be affected by it. And as you comprehend the beauty of this life, deep down, *you* want to be like that as well. One person's humility inspires another's. How much more is this the case when we set our eyes on Christ!

This is nowhere more true than with the sight of Christ humbling himself on the cross. At the foot of the cross, our sin is revealed—we are killed—God's grace is revealed—we are brought to new life. We only enjoy grace when we recognize what sinners we are. As soon as you vainly forget how great a sinner you are, God's grace will cease to amaze you. This is a good litmus test of your spiritual health: Are you still amazed by his grace? Once you've tasted God's grace, you don't want to forget your sinfulness entirely, because your sinfulness accentuates his mercy.

At the cross, we develop honesty. When we stray from the cross, vanity and deceitfulness creep back in. But when we return to the cross, we don't want to pretend to be perfect or better than we are. We want the grace that is only for the failures.

At the cross, we develop graciousness. Having received grace, we become gracious. There we grow compassion for others in their stumbling. And by crushing our deluded pride, the cross enables us to allow others to flourish. When I am standing at the foot of the cross, I don't have to keep others down or compete. I want their gifts to shine.

With this I will close: power is given to us *that we might serve others.* And so, if I might sound for a moment like Oliver Cromwell, I beseech you in the bowels of Christ: seek to grow in Christ. And to do that, keep close to the cross.

5

Esteem Friendship

*"Two are better than one, because they have a good re-
ward for their toil. For if they fall, one will lift up his fellow. But woe to him who is alone when he falls and has not
another to lift him up! Again, if two lie together, they keep
warm, but how can one keep warm alone? And though
a man might prevail against one who is alone, two will
withstand him—a threefold cord is not quickly broken."*

– Ecclesiastes 4:9–12

Today, we're all swimming downstream from Thomas
Carlyle. Thomas Carlyle, that great nineteenth-
century historian and polymath, is famous for his "great
men of history" theory. Here's how he explained it:

> Universal History, the history of what man has accom-
> plished in this world, is at bottom the History of the

> Great Men who have worked here. They were the lead-
> ers of men, these great ones; the modellers, patterns,
> and in a wide sense creators, of whatsoever the general
> mass of men contrived to do or to attain... In all epochs
> of the world's history, we shall find the Great Man to
> have been the indispensable savior of his epoch;—the
> lightning, without which the fuel never would have
> burnt. The History of the World, I said already, was the
> Biography of Great Men.[1]

In other words, as Carlyle saw it, history is steered and shaped by—in fact, history *is*—Caesar, Charlemagne, Napoleon, Washington. Our thoughts are shaped by great men: Plato, Newton, Nietzsche, Darwin, Marx. And as Christians, the way we look at church history and his-torical theology can feed that. We sometimes approach these topics as a survey of theological and pastoral greats: Athanasius, Augustine, Aquinas, Luther, Calvin, Edwards.

And make no mistake, I really want to spend time with those men—and if you are a good student of church history, you certainly will! But there is also a danger in this

---

1 Thomas Carlyle, *Heroes and Hero-Worship* (London & New York: Ward, Lock, and Co., 1888), 3, 11.

approach—namely, that we would gather the impression that the growth of the church is all about great men.

And it's not just in studying history that this is a temptation: the church itself can become a "great men" culture. Think of the appeal of the big name in conferences; think of all those names on the backs of the books we buy; think of whose circles you want to be in and whose name you want to cite: "He was my teacher" or "I shared a meal with him once." Think of how we use big names to win an argument, to support our own point of view.

I'm not suggesting that this is all wrong. There's something right about having leaders we trust. But for young would-be leaders going into church ministry, there is a danger in this hierarchical, "focus-on-the-individual" kind of thinking. It can distort your ambitions. After all, you rightfully want to be fruitful—and if that's how God works, through great men, then you will also want to be a great man.

It's not just that your gospel vision can skew into a desire for personal greatness; the "great men" theory can set you on a course to being a lone ranger. A hero. A splendid, solitary oak tree—marvelous in its aloneness, something to be admired from afar.

But one of the greatest practical problems I see across the church is the isolation of so many church leaders. There are many contributing factors, but surely one of them is the idea that spiritual growth occurs only or mainly through the purposeful, influential actions of elevated individuals.

Please let me be clear: I don't want to downplay the genius of many great men. Throughout church history, and even in the biblical narratives, it has often been an exceptional man raised up by God who has provided the special leadership or reform the church has needed. Surely we see that in a Luther, a Lloyd-Jones, a Stott, and others.

But even when the church has had one of those great men, these men have never been alone. In fact, it is precisely when they are alone that the problems occur. Indeed, all through church history, collegiality has ever been central to times of spiritual blessing.

For instance, in theology, think of the galaxy of friends around Augustine, Luther, Calvin. In mission, our minds can quickly leap to a missionary hero like William Carey, but we fail to remember the circle of friends around him: Andrew Fuller, John Sutcliff, Samuel Pearce, and John Ryland. Or take Billy Graham. Just as Carey would never have been Carey without those friends, so Billy Graham would not have been the Billy Graham we know without

Cliff Barrows, George Beverly Shea, the Wilsons, and Leighton Ford.

I think of how John Stott loved to go away on writing breaks here in Wales with Dick Lucas and Richard Bewes and of how he would deliberately nurture others in turn. Yes, again and again in church history, we see that it is a band of brothers who gather together around a shared vision. They're not merely acquaintances or colleagues; they're friends, and they encourage and push each other on.

And sometimes in these bands of brothers we recognize that there was no leading great man at all. Think of the Puritans: in a sense, yes, there were many great men among the Puritans, many well-positioned to shape and raise new leaders. But it wasn't a movement built around one man. It was a movement and fellowship that grew out of a broadly shared vision.

C. S. Lewis said in *The Four Loves* that where lovers look into each others' eyes, friends stand "side by side" and look ahead to their "common interest."[2] This imagery brings to mind the seraphim in Isaiah's vision, crying "Holy, holy, holy" *to one another* (Isa. 6:3).

This is why we started Reformation Fellowship: to gather friends around a shared passion.

---

2 C. S. Lewis, *The Four Loves* (London, Geoffrey Bles, 1960), 73.

Now, it's actually slightly unusual to talk about friendship like this in Christian circles. We talk about "networks." We talk about "fellowship." But both can be quite relationally hollow or chilly phrases. To "network" can be just to use a contact to get something done, or to make a superficial connection now that we hope might pay off in some way later. "Fellowship" is often nothing more than Christians drinking coffee together. Or sometimes we truly do fellowship in Christ, working together for the sake of the gospel.

We should aim higher. Psalm 133 sings of "how good and pleasant it is when brothers dwell in unity" (v. 1). It is like oil running down the beard of the high priest at his ordination or like the dew that rolls down the mountains of Zion, making the land fruitful (vv. 2–3). Appropriately, in his High Priestly prayer in John 17, Jesus prayed to his Father that "that they may be one even as we are one" (v. 22). For as the oil ran down from Aaron's head to his body, so the Spirit runs down from Christ our Head to his Body, the church. Our oneness is a Spirit-wrought reflection on earth of a heavenly beauty.

Warm and hearty friendship is the highest form of fellowship. It is an anticipation of what fellowship will be like in heaven. It is partnership, allying together in warm, rich, personal appreciation. This sort of fellowship testifies to a friendly, personal God and an eternal hope where all the fellowship involves true and holy delight.

I mentioned C. S. Lewis' *The Four Loves*: I wonder if you've read it? If you haven't, you've got a treat to enjoy sometime. His chapter on friendship is a favorite of mine. It's an insight-packed paean to friendship.

Interestingly, one of the first points Lewis makes is that institutions often dislike and distrust friendship: "Its leaders very often do. Headmasters and Headmistresses and Heads of religious communities, colonels and ships' captains, can feel uneasy when close and strong friendships arise between … their subjects."[3]

But there's no need to distrust it, for a friendship is not the same thing as an exclusive coterie or cabal. "True Friendship," says Lewis, "is the least jealous of loves. Two friends delight to be joined by a third, and three by a fourth, if only the newcomer is qualified to become a real friend."[4]

The foundation for friendship, Lewis says, is companionship, which is what we often mean by the term "fellowship." He writes, "I prefer to call it Companionship

---

3 Lewis, *Four Loves*, 70.
4 Lewis, *Four Loves*, 74.

or Clubbableness." Companionship entails a basic willingness to get on and work well with others.

Companionship is a necessary starting point. But that's still not quite friendship. "Friendship," Lewis adds,

> arises out of mere Companionship when two or more of the companions discover that they have in common some insight or interest… That is why those pathetic people who simply "want friends" can never make any. The very condition of having Friends is that we should want something else besides Friends. Where … I only want a Friend, no Friendship can arise.[5]

In other words, it takes the shared interest to create the friendship. The one enables the other.

Then, Lewis goes on to see what this friendship is that shared interest has created. And he argues that friends are not just allies; they're not just useful when the times are tough. Friend means more than that: "Friendship is unnecessary, like philosophy, like art, like the universe itself (for God did not need to create). It has no survival value; rather it is one of those things which give value to survival."[6]

---

5 Lewis, *Four Loves*, 77, 79.

6 Lewis, *Four Loves*, 84.

That is, friendship is not a means to an end but an end, a value, in itself—something which enriches our humanity. So what has happened is that the common quest or vision which unites the Friends has not absorbed them in such a way that they remain ignorant or oblivious of one another. Through their common vision, they become blessed with an affection for each other.

You see this, for example, in the friendship of John Newton and William Cowper. They found their friendship in their shared desire to produce hymns for the church. But that shared quest brought something more. Here were two quite broken men—Newton with a painful past, Cowper with his depression—supporting each other personally, protecting each other, and bringing the best out of each other.

And hear Lewis on what it's like to be in such a friendship circle:

> In a perfect Friendship this Appreciative love is, I think, often so great and so firmly based that each member of the circle feels, in his secret heart, humbled before all the rest. Sometimes he wonders what he is doing there among his betters. He is lucky beyond desert to be in such company. Especially when the whole group is together, each bringing out all that is best, wisest, or

funniest in all the others. Those are the golden sessions; when four or five of us after a hard day's walking have come to our inn; when our slippers are on, our feet spread out towards the blaze and our drinks at our elbows; when the whole world, and something beyond the world, opens itself to our minds as we talk; and no one has any claim on or any responsibility for another, but all are free-men and equals as if we had first met an hour ago, while at the same time an Affection mellowed by the years enfolds us. Life—natural life—has no better gift to give. Who could have deserved it?[7]

That's the wonder of friendship: it opens our eyes to know another and so to appreciate them as themselves. We see behind their role and their potential usefulness: we see them and begin to sympathize with their weaknesses and esteem them for their qualities.

It is for us in our Friendships as it was for Christiana and her party in *The Pilgrim's Progress*:

They seemed to be a terror one to the other, for that they could not see that glory each one on herself which they could see in each other. Now therefore they began

7 Lewis, *Four Loves*, 85.

to esteem each other better than themselves. For you are
fairer than I am, said one; and you are more comely than
I am, said another.[8]

This isn't politeness or flattery: friendship opens our eyes to
the qualities and beauties in our friends.

At the end of the first chapter of his letter to the Philippians, Paul wrote a passionate plea:

Only let your manner of life be worthy of the gospel of
Christ, *so that* whether I come and see you or am absent,
I may hear of you that you are standing firm in one spirit, with one mind striving side by side for the faith of the
gospel. (Phil. 1:27, emphasis added)

Notice his logic: living "worthy of the gospel of Christ"
must include "with one mind striving side by side for the
faith of the gospel." When the Son of Man is lifted up, he
draws people *together* to himself (see John 12:32). A culture
of individual isolation and lone rangers is not a culture of
the gospel.

---

8 John Bunyan, *The Pilgrim's Progress from This World to That Which Is to Come*, in
The Works of John Bunyan, vol. 3, *Allegorical, Figurative, and Symbolical* (Edinburgh,
Banner of Truth, 1991), 190.

The gospel creates a taste of heaven that is fruitful on earth: an anticipation of that day in heaven when, like the seraphim, we cry to each other in affectionate shared adoration: "Holy, holy, holy is the LORD of hosts; the whole earth is full of his glory!"

6

Grow through Suffering

"Beloved, do not be surprised at the fiery trial when it comes upon you to test you, as though something strange were happening to you. But rejoice insofar as you share Christ's sufferings." – 1 Peter 4:12–13

Modern thought about suffering tends to be afflicted by an infection that's gone deeper in the West than most realize: deep in our psyche is the assumption that we are entitled. Entitled to what? To health, wealth, and prosperity.

In contrast, Peter can urge us to *rejoice* in our sufferings not because he's a religious masochist, but because he knows: Christ is the firstborn, our forerunner, and where he goes, we follow. He is our Head, and like in a birth, the body must follow where the head goes. This is the pathway through suffering to glory.

Everyone suffers, gets ill, and grows old, but for the Christian, all of this is changed. For us, none of this is pointless. Born again into Christ's new humanity, we've been taken out of the simple downward slide into death. That's the horror for the unbeliever: it's all downhill. Things are only going to get worse—old age, then death, and then they hope *against* hope that maybe there is something more.

But for us, we've been taken out of that, brought into Christ's life. We share *his* direction of travel now. "Rejoice insofar as you share Christ's sufferings, that you may also rejoice and be glad when his glory is revealed. If you are insulted for the name of Christ, you are blessed, because the Spirit of glory and of God rests upon you" (1 Pet. 4:13–14).

And Peter's no hypocrite as he addresses us. In Acts 5, Peter and the apostles were flogged before the Sanhedrin, yet they left, we are told, "rejoicing because they had been counted worthy to suffer dishonor for the name"—the dear name of Jesus (v. 41). It wasn't that the flogging didn't hurt. It was that their desire to be like Jesus was stronger. There was joy to be found sharing in the sufferings of Christ.

This is worth pressing into. Think of the very first time the suffering of Christ gets spoken of in the Bible: Where would you place this? It is in Genesis 3:15, where the Lord says to the serpent, "I will put enmity between you and the woman, and between your offspring and her offspring; he shall bruise your head, and you shall bruise his heel."

That, of course, tells us about *the* offspring, *the* seed: Christ, the promised Son. But Paul picks up the verse and says it can apply also to Christians: "The God of peace will soon crush Satan under your feet" (Rom. 16:20). Do you see what Paul has done? He's saying that we're brought into Christ bruised and bruising. "He shall bruise your head, and you shall bruise his heel."

Paul speaks here of the special bruising Christ's people must go through. We become united with the Bruised One. Where once we were at peace with the god of this world, where once we loved how he blinded us (we loved how he covered us with darkness because it hid our shame), now our eyes have been opened, and we've come out from under his dark dominion. Our old master is angry with us.

And so are his offspring, that is, all who still follow the prince of the power of the air. As we turning to love Christ, sometimes friends, family, and outright foes start to portray us as weird, fanatical, a threat. A war has begun. And we feel it in our bones. Sin, which once was so purely sweet to us, has lost its sweetness. It chafes, and we want to be free of what we once loved. Yet we are also under attack, and there are impediments to our progress in Christ.

The world, the flesh, the devil: of course Christians are going to suffer! But look at the counterweight that Paul gives us: "The God of peace will soon crush Satan under your feet." Yes, we're brought into Christ bruised. But we are also brought into Christ bruising. Yes, we will get bruised as we follow Christ, but consider what bruising we'll do in his power and his name!

And that's the perspective all of Scripture wants to give us: never triumphalistic, but definitely triumphant—even in the day of small things, even in the day of being bruised. Scripture urges us: Don't be naive; do be deeply jubilant. Satan nibbles at our feet, but we crush his head. We are heading to glory, but even as we are bruised now, with our great firstborn Brother, we do some bruising.

As Christians suffer patiently, like Christ; as we are content when all the world is so unsatisfied; as we walk away from the glittering rubbish of the world—we show that all the world does not satisfy; we show how Satan has been stripped of his power. Every time we rejoice in Christ, resist sin, proclaim him, and show his love, we do something completely unnatural. We show our freedom from the serpent's chains. We stomp on the old dragon's head.

Our passage in 1 Peter focuses us on Christ's glory. But before we get to see how secure and how superb is this glory, we need to see a bit more how we can "rejoice," as Peter says, in the sufferings we will face. Verse 14 reads, "If you are insulted for the name of Christ, you are blessed, because the Spirit of glory and of God rests upon you." Think on that one: if you're insulted for Christ, it proves you're standing with Christ. Verse 15: "But let none of you suffer as a murderer or a thief or an evildoer or as a meddler." In other words, just because you've sinned or you've acted like an idiot doesn't mean you can dress up your suffering as though it were part of spiritual growth. You can't get a ticket for speeding and then come to church saying, "Look at me; I'm suffering for Christ!"

The passage continues:

> Yet if anyone suffers as a Christian, let him not be ashamed, but let him glorify God in that name. For it is time for judgment to begin at the household of God; and if it begins with us, what will be the outcome for those who do not obey the gospel of God? And
> "If the righteous is scarcely saved,
>   what will become of the ungodly and the sinner?"
> Therefore let those who suffer according to God's will entrust their souls to a faithful Creator while doing good. (vv. 16–19)

What does the phrase "it is time for judgment to begin at the household of God" mean? The point is this: our wonderful Father is about removing all that is foul and evil from his world—death, sin, wickedness. He judged it all at the cross. One day the fire of his wrath will envelop the world, and he will cleanse it completely. For now, the fire of his judgment burns mostly among his people, whom he has baptized with Spirit and fire (see Luke 3:16).

The term "judgment" is usually one that we shy away from. And it's true that for those who love sin and don't want Christ, that fire of God's judgment is purely terrible. But for us who love Christ, it is entirely different. Our sinful identity and status have already been put to death on the cross. Sin is no longer our identity; so when we are put through the fire, we are not consumed; rather—as Peter puts it in 1:7—we are like gold refined. Not us but our sin is burned up.

While being refined by fire is never comfortable, it's just what we want, isn't it? Whenever we think on Christ, we see: of course he is better than my sin. His pure and loving ways are freedom, life, and light. "Lord, cleanse me," we cry, for we would be like Jesus!

Suffering is not something that we actively seek. Yet times of suffering can be amazingly fruitful. My own experience has been that suffering has always taught me far more than ease. I don't always understand what I'm going through at the time, or why, but as I look back, I am so grateful for what the Lord has led me through: trial has left me less attached to old addictions; more contented; so much more joyful and free.

Sometimes when we encounter suffering, we set our sights too low. We simply hope to endure. But even under intense affliction, a Christian can actually do more than cope; a Christian, Peter teaches, can actually profit from suffering. This is only true because Christians are the children of an omnipotent and loving Father. Even our trials are in his kind hands.

This vision of suffering is a startlingly different way of seeing the world than how we naturally think, and it's one with a very different idea of what "the good life" is. Ease and prosperity in and of themselves are not really what make up the good life. Through external pleasures, Satan can bring about internal devastation.

That being the case, God is not sadistic or heartless when he brings about hard providences for his people. Hebrews 12 puts it famously: "My son, do not regard lightly the discipline of the Lord, nor be weary when reproved by him. For the Lord disciplines the one he loves" (vv. 5–6). If we are the brothers and sisters of the one who was made perfect through suffering, then our Father will use suffering to perfect us, to make us like Jesus. Hard providences are, for us, no longer marks of condemning judgment, but marks of paternal care that flow from the concern of the Father.

Our lives are like a pond: when all is calm, we can look quite pure and clear. Then along comes unsettling trouble, and all the mud at the bottom of our souls comes up: we're exposed for what we really are. God unsettles his saints to expose the evil within—so that it might be removed.

If trials can be beneficial for all believers, they are invaluable for gospel ministers who must lead God's people through suffering. We do this not just by our teaching, but by our lives; our lives enflesh and prove our doctrine. The life and faithfulness of the Christian leader preaches a loud lesson to the people about finding comfort in God amid trials.

Spurgeon describes the role of suffering in the life of a pastor like this:

> Uninterrupted success and unfading joy in it would be more than our weak heads could bear. Our wine must needs be mixed with water, lest it turn our brains. My witness is, that those who are honoured of their Lord in public, have usually to endure a secret chastening, or

to carry a peculiar cross, lest by any means they exalt themselves, and fall into the snare of the devil.[1]

Christ himself was made like his weak and tempted brothers in order that he might help those who are tempted (Heb. 2:16–18), and in the same manner, it is weak and suffering people that God has chosen to minister to the weak and suffering. Angels or superhumans simply could not sympathize with human groans; their very strength would only mock our weakness and thus mock the gospel.

All told, said Spurgeon, the "rod of God teacheth us more than all the voices of his ministers."[2] Strong words indeed from one with so high a view of preaching!

The great Refiner uses the days of small things. He uses the setbacks and discouragements, and even severe suffering, for our ultimate blessing. He did just that at the cross: it was through that darkest and most discouraging day that he definitively overturned and defeated the very root of darkness and suffering. Through that death he defeated death; through our *comparatively* light sufferings he is

---

1 C. H. Spurgeon, *Lectures to My Students: A Selection from Addresses Delivered to the Students of the Pastors' College, Metropolitan Tabernacle.*, vol. 1 (London: Passmore and Alabaster, 1875), 178.

2 C. H. Spurgeon, *The Metropolitan Tabernacle Pulpit Sermons*, vol. 22 (London: Passmore & Alabaster, 1876), 76.

able to defeat our selfish independence and our foolish wandering and to make us more like his free and victorious Son.

For those who have even glimpsed the unfettered beauty of Jesus, that thought itself puts mettle in our joy. After all, having seen in him what it looks like to be free of sin's shriveling power, we want to be like him!

Recognizing this, the Puritan John Flavel was strongly inclined to see sunshine behind all clouds of sorrow. That optimism he captured in a little poem:

> If Satan could see the issue, and th' event
> Of his temptations, he would scarcely tempt.
> Could saints but see what fruits their troubles bring,
> Amidst those troubles they would shout and sing.
> O sacred wisdom! who can but admire
> To see how thou dost save from fire, by fire!
> No doubt but saints in glory wond'ring stand
> At those strange methods few now understand.[3]

And yet, in the midst of suffering, Flavel knew how hard it can be to believe there is sun behind the clouds. He knew that suffering doesn't automatically sanctify the sufferer;

---

3 John Flavel, *The Whole Works of John Flavel*, vol. 5 (London: W. Baynes and Son, 1820), 281.

under suffering we can become more bitter, angry, despairing. Instead of presenting our complaints *to* God, which is good, we can complain *of* God and turn against him.

Flavel gives this advice to those who are suffering: look to Scripture. What we pass through will make no sense and will most assuredly incline us to despair unless the Word of God is a lamp to our feet in the darkness. Only when Scripture shapes our response to suffering can we profit from it and grow in Christian liberty and Christlikeness.

A second important response when we encounter suffering is to look to God. When life is turned upside down and all seems terrifyingly uncertain, "Eye the immutability of God; look on him as the rock of ages... It may be two or three days hath made a sad change in your condition: the death of a dear relation hath turned all things upside down... O how composing are those views of God to our spirits under dark providences."[4] When all seems broken, uncertain, or wrong, remember God the unchanging who, through it all, cannot be broken, uncertain, or wrong.

Peter has given us guidance about something the world cannot understand: how to rejoice in the hard and discouraging times. Let me as clear as I can: Peter talks

---

4 John Flavel, *The Whole Works of John Flavel*, vol. 4 (London: W. Baynes and Son, 1820), 426–27.

about suffering, then glory—but that does not mean that we experience suffering first, and only then joy. No, solid, grounded joy is what will get you *through* suffering. For Christ and his people, joy precedes, follows, underlies, and encases all suffering. Christ had joy before all pain, before the world existed. And it was joy that strengthened his resolve then to suffer (Heb. 12:2). That is what he shares with us: a preceding joy that enables us to bear hardship.

It is the happy secret of the saints who have borne hardship most cheerfully and bravely for Christ: the more we find our pleasure in him, the more willing we will then be to suffer with him. As the happy old Puritan Richard Sibbes put it: "We will not suffer with him, if we will not feast with him; we will not suffer with him, if we will not joy with him, and in him."[5]

And something that helps here is to know: Christ is not just the one who is powerful enough to bring us, at last, beyond our sufferings. He is also the one who has gone through suffering. He understands. He has compassion now on his beloved ones who are struggling. He groaned with pity over the leper when he was on earth. He was

---

5 Richard Sibbes, *The Complete Works of Richard Sibbes*, ed. Alexander Balloch Grosart, vol. 2 (Edinburgh; London; Dublin: James Nichol; James Nisbet and Co.; W. Robertson, 1862), 34–35.

moved by the harassed and the helpless. And just so is he now in heaven: he sympathizes with our weaknesses.

But of course, darkness is not where the Bible leaves things, and neither should we. We must move on from looking at rejoicing in the discouraging and hard days to this "exceeding joy" (1 Pet. 4:13 KJV), this exultation "when his glory is revealed."

The first thing you need to know and be clear on about Christ's glory is a wonderful Reformation insight: this glory is certain. Secure. Steadfast. He is in glory now, and one day all the world will see it. And as surely as Christ is in glory, his own must join him. The head cannot have glory without the body. The Bridegroom does not keep his status and his riches to himself.

The accuser loves to have people doubt this. He loves to whisper: "God is punishing you. That's why things are hard. He doesn't love you anymore." And we must shout back, "Satan, what sort of Christ do you think I have? A faithless Christ? One who makes all depend on me? No, I have one who says 'no one will snatch them out of my hand'" (see John 10:28).

By our nature, and sometimes succumbing to the attacks of the enemy, we are quick to take suffering to mean that God is against us or has somehow weakened in his love and care for us. But that is not so. Nothing in Scripture supports this interpretation of suffering. Instead, we learn from the whole counsel of God that suffering is part of his plan for our redemption and sanctification. If he does not condemn us, on what grounds can we condemn ourselves?

This is one reason that the doctrine of justification is something that we can lean on whenever we face the discouragements of suffering. If we forget that we are justified by faith through grace, every trial becomes a double trial; we increase our suffering as we wonder if God hates us. We take on burdens that we were never meant to carry.

The doctrine of justification lifts our burdens when we come to Jesus for salvation; it also alleviates the weight of false guilt or false responsibility that can overcome us during seasons of difficulty.

Perhaps you have heard the phrase "There, but for the grace of God, go I." These words are often attributed to the English Reformer John Bradford, who reportedly said them while watching prisoners being led to their execution. Death, he knew, was what his sin deserved. The only thing standing between him and death was God's grace.

Bradford penned a collection of meditations to be used throughout the day, applying the gospel to life. For the moments as we prepare to go to sleep, he says, "As you are not afraid to enter into your bed … so be not afraid to die."[6] More certain than waking from our sleep, we shall awake and rise up from death in that happy morning.

Bradford proved the depth of his confidence when he was forty-five years old. He was sentenced to be burned to death at Smithfield as part of "Bloody" Queen Mary's campaign against the evangelicals. Tied to the stake, he turned to his fellow martyr, John Leaf, and said, "Be of good comfort, brother; for we shall have a merry supper with the Lord this night." Bradford knew: our momentary afflictions are light. The weight of eternal glory is great (2 Cor. 4:17).

Friends, rejoice and share this hope through all trials. And in all you face, fix your eyes on Jesus, our forerunner, who for the joy set before him endured the cross, despising the shame, and is seated, beckoning, at the right hand of the throne of God.

---

6 John Bradford, *The Writings of John Bradford*, ed. Aubrey Townsend, vol. 1, *Sermons, Meditations, Examinations* (Cambridge: Cambridge University Press, 1848), 241.

7

Love the Church

"For Zion's sake I will not keep silent,
and for Jerusalem's sake I will not be quiet,
until her righteousness goes forth as brightness,
and her salvation as a burning torch." – Isaiah 62:1

We will never be Christlike if we do not love and serve Christ's church. The church is why the cosmos exists. Jonathan Edwards put it like this:

> The creation of the world seems to have been especially for this end, that the eternal Son of God might obtain a spouse, towards whom he might fully exercise the infinite benevolence of his nature, and to whom he might, as it were, open and pour forth all that immense fountain of condescension, love, and grace that was in his heart, and that in this way God might be glorified.[1]

---

1 Jonathan Edwards, *Works of Jonathan Edwards*, ed. Wilson H. Kimnach, vol. 25, *Sermons and Discourses* (New Haven and London: Yale University Press, 2006), 187.

This is nothing more than the sweet biblical theme of election: God created so that the eternal Son of God might have a bride to enjoy and share his all with, so that he could shower on her the oceans of love that were in his heart.

God made us for the Son. He also saved us for the Son. Why did the Son endure the cross? "For the joy that was set before him," we're told in Hebrews 12:2. What joy? Why, surely it's the joy of what the cross would finally achieve. Listen to the words of Revelation 19:7: "Let us rejoice and exult and give him the glory, for the marriage of the Lamb has come, and his Bride"—the church—"has made herself ready."

That's the final end Jesus worked and bled for: "the holy city, new Jerusalem, coming down out of heaven from God, *prepared as a bride adorned for her husband*" (Rev. 21:2, emphasis added). Everything he does is for her. She is his passion, his motivation, his delight.

Let's press into this now with a look at Isaiah 61 and 62. The verses in question—61:10 to 62:5—span two chapters, but they actually comprise a single seven-line stanza in the middle of one of Isaiah's songs of the Messiah. We have to look back to 61:1 in order to see who's speaking here. "The Spirit of the Lord God is upon me, because the Lord has anointed me to bring good news to the poor." These are the words of the anointed one, the Messiah.

In verse 10, the speaker is full of rejoicing. He's clothed in salvation. He's covered with a beautiful robe of righteousness. He's ornamented "as a bridegroom." What for? "For," 61:11—or "because"—he wants something like a fruitful garden to grow. This isn't just a garden full of plants. Rather, "righteousness and praise" will "sprout up before all the nations." And how will this happen?

Let's keep reading. At the start of chapter 62, the same speaker says,

> For Zion's sake I will not keep silent,
>   and for Jerusalem's sake I will not be quiet,
> until her righteousness goes forth as brightness,
>   and her salvation as a burning torch.

Whose righteousness inspires the Messiah to rejoice? Who will shine the light of praise to all the nations? None other than Zion, Jerusalem, the holy city where God dwells. She is prepared as a bride. All of the Bridegroom's preparation is about her, is for her. He makes himself ready, and his purpose is the church.

The speaker then shifts to address the bride: "The nations shall see your righteousness, and all the kings your glory" (v. 2). As noted above, the Bridegroom "will not keep quiet." He will not rest, he will not stop, he will not relent until his bride is glorified and all the world gasps at her beauty.

We who love the church but also see so keenly her faults need to hear this. Those of us who labor in the vineyards may look at the church and see a marginalized and messed-up community. We may think it insignificant (at least in others' eyes) or weak. But this is the Lord Christ's bride: he will come, and he will take her to himself. He will vindicate her, heal her, glorify her.

But what does it mean for the church to be married to Christ? Let's look first at all the language of "righteousness" here. In 61:10, he says that the Lord has covered *him* with a robe of righteousness. But then in 62:1, he says he's going to cause *her* righteousness to go forth as brightness; he's going to ensure, verse 2, that nations see *her* righteousness. He's righteous, and now she's seen as righteous.

This is nothing less than the gospel! This is just what Martin Luther rediscovered in the Reformation, and he explained it like this. Luther told the story of a king (representing Jesus) marrying a poor girl—in fact, a prostitute (representing us). And at their wedding day, she says to him: "All that I am I give to you, and all that I have I share with you!" And so, she shares with him all her debts and shame. And the king says, "And all that I am I give to you, and all that I have I share with you." And with those words, he is hers: she becomes a queen, and all his kingdom is hers.

"All that I have I share with you." That is the great marriage swap of the gospel. Our great Bridegroom has taken all our sin, our death, our judgment; and he has shared with us all his perfect righteousness. He takes our sin; we take his righteousness. And so, said Luther, the sinner can confidently display "her sins in the face of death and hell and say, 'If I have sinned, yet my Christ, in whom I believe, has not sinned, and all his is mine and all mine is his.'"[2]

Because we are united to Christ in this marriage, we too can share those words: "I will greatly rejoice in the LORD; my soul shall exult in my God, for he has clothed me with the garments of salvation; he has covered me with the robe of righteousness … as a bride adorns herself with her jewels" (Isa. 61:10).

For the church to be the bride of Christ means that she is righteous in his sight. But it's far more: see how proud of her he is. He wants her to be an object of wonder. He wants all the nations, all the world, to see her beauty. Notice all the light language in these verses: brightness, a burning torch, glory. It's like she's a second sun in the sky— so glorious that even kings will look. Even their glory will

---

2 To George Spenlein, in *Luther: Letters of Spiritual Counsel*, Library of Christian Classics, ed. T. G Tappert (Vancouver: Regent College, 2003), 110.

not compare to hers. Their eyes will be torn away from themselves to gaze on her.

In fact, Isaiah 62:3 says, "You shall be a crown of beauty in the hand of the LORD, and a royal diadem in the hand of your God." That's God's design: finding this people, this church, sprawling in the dirt, wretched and helpless, he picks her up, gives her a new name, and cleans, beautifies, and transforms her to be a "crown of beauty," a "royal diadem" in his hand.

A crown is a most precious treasure; it is a reward for great victors and conquerors. It is the sign of greatest honor for its bearer. Paul uses this term when he writes to the Philippians, calling them "my brothers, whom I love and long for, my joy *and crown*" (Phil. 4:1, emphasis added). They are his reward, and a sign of his faithful apostleship. Proverbs 12:4 says, "An excellent wife is the crown of her husband."

The church is the excellent wife, the crown of Jesus Christ. The church is his most precious treasure, the reward for his great victory; it is the sign of just who he is. He is the one who awakens the dead, saves the helpless, and draws mankind together in love.

In the church is displayed—for all the world to see—a divine glory. She is a taste of heaven come to earth. But there's something even more, as we read in verses 4–5:

You shall no more be termed Forsaken,
    and your land shall no more be termed Desolate,
but you shall be called My Delight Is in Her,
    and your land Married;
for the Lord delights in you,
    and your land shall be married.
For as a young man marries a young woman,
    so shall your sons marry you,
and as the bridegroom rejoices over the bride,
    so shall your God rejoice over you.

Jesus Christ has the most passionate love for—*delight in*—his bride. She thrills him. She's not earned his favor and salvation. But in her he has created something that makes his pupils dilate, that makes his heart skip a beat.

The nature of Christ's desire for the church means three things for us. First, we cannot be separated from or unconcerned about the church. John Owen put it this way: "Living interaction with saints and believers is essential to the student. It will sharpen, by exercise and practice, those spiritual gifts on which true gospel wisdom is founded, and that wisdom itself will be strengthened and increased by the holy practice. Such service is the essential inner nature of theology itself."[3]

---

3 John Owen, *Biblical Theology, or the Nature, Origin, Development, and Study of Theological Truth, in Six Books*, trans. Stephen P. Westcott (Pittsburgh: Soli Deo Gloria, 1994), 703.

Second, if the church is Christ's beloved bride, we must treat her with great respect. It's so tempting to want the church to look at us, to admire us, to depend on us. But think what that is! Richard Sibbes said, "Many make love to the spouse of Christ."[4] Trying to get the bride to admire you is flirting with the bride of Christ. True friends do not behave that way. No, if we're friends of Christ, we point the church to her husband.

Third and last, if we love Christ, we will share his concerns. We will mirror his actions as a champion of his bride, adding our voice to his words in Isaiah 62:1. Resolve with him now: "For Zion's sake I [too] will not keep silent, and for Jerusalem's sake I [too] will not be quiet, until her righteousness goes forth as brightness, and her salvation as a burning torch."

These are not merely beautiful words that are spoken in a moment of sincere but fleeting passion for the bride. We can see the utmost seriousness of these words when we consider the earlier chapters in Isaiah, particularly Isaiah 53.

Take a moment to revisit the lovely, familiar words of chapter 53. These is the lengths to which he will go on behalf of his beloved. This is how much he cherishes the church.

---

4 Richard Sibbes, *The Complete Works of Richard Sibbes*, ed. Alexander Balloch Grosart, vol. 2 (Edinburgh; London; Dublin: James Nichol; James Nisbet and Co.; W. Robertson, 1862), 202.

He was despised and rejected by men,

    a man of sorrows and acquainted with grief;

and as one from whom men hide their faces

    he was despised, and we esteemed him not.

Surely he has borne our griefs

    and carried our sorrows;

yet we esteemed him stricken,

    smitten by God, and afflicted.

But he was pierced for our transgressions;

    he was crushed for our iniquities;

upon him was the chastisement that brought us peace,

    and with his wounds we are healed.

All we like sheep have gone astray;

    we have turned—every one—to his own way;

and the LORD has laid on him

    the iniquity of us all.

He was oppressed, and he was afflicted,

    yet he opened not his mouth;

like a lamb that is led to the slaughter,

    and like a sheep that before its shearers is silent,

    so he opened not his mouth.

By oppression and judgment he was taken away;

and as for his generation, who considered

that he was cut off out of the land of the living,

stricken for the transgression of my people?

And they made his grave with the wicked

and with a rich man in his death,

although he had done no violence,

and there was no deceit in his mouth.

Yet it was the will of the LORD to crush him;

he has put him to grief;

when his soul makes an offering for guilt,

he shall see his offspring; he shall prolong his days;

the will of the LORD shall prosper in his hand.

Out of the anguish of his soul he shall see and be satisfied;

by his knowledge shall the righteous one, my servant,

make many to be accounted righteous,

and he shall bear their iniquities.

Therefore I will divide him a portion with the many,

and he shall divide the spoil with the strong,

because he poured out his soul to death

and was numbered with the transgressors;

yet he bore the sin of many,

and makes intercession for the transgressors. (vv. 3–12)

Now, what is a fit response to such a Savior? Isaiah 54 reveals it:

> "Sing, O barren one, who did not bear;
>> break forth into singing and cry aloud,
>> you who have not been in labor!
> For the children of the desolate one will be more
>> than the children of her who is married," says the LORD.
> "Enlarge the place of your tent,
>> and let the curtains of your habitations be stretched out;
> do not hold back; lengthen your cords
>> and strengthen your stakes.
> For you will spread abroad to the right and to the left,
>> and your offspring will possess the nations
>> and will people the desolate cities." (vv. 1–3)

What does this vision of the Savior's love compel in us? With such a Bridegroom, we are not to hunker down and cower at the secularization of the culture or its anti-Christian armory. Instead, we are to sing. We are to enlarge the tent, for we will spread abroad to the right and to the left (Isa. 54:2–3).

We sing and we enlarge the church because the death of Christ means the life of the church. He suffers, and his church flourishes. She is the one he died for. The growing church is his hard-earned reward, his glory. He suffered and died so that his church, his people, might fill the earth and inherit it. Whenever the church is full of this good news of Jesus, it grows.

It was this passage in Isaiah 54 that the great missionary William Carey preached before leaving England to take the gospel to India. Seeking to stir the church to global mission, this is what he said to them: "Expect great things from God. Attempt great things for God."

How can we expect or attempt less? Christ's concern for the church—that she spread out, that she shine before the world like a crown of beauty—this is a passion that can capture the greatest heart and inspire the greatest mind. This is not a petty dream; this is the desire and delight of God's own Son. It is his definitive passion and purpose; nothing else can top it.

If you long to share the most beautiful, the most significant, the most delightful passion there is, share this: the church holding out the glory of Christ. This is our guiding passion and joy until the coming day when we will sit down together at the marriage supper of the Lamb, in endless joy.

8

Be a Theologian,
But Take Care

"Test everything; hold fast what is good."

– 1 Thessalonians 5:21

To be human is to be a theologian, for everyone has a god.

To understand this, we are going to need to re-examine our working definition of "theology." We will need to rescue it from the idea that it is just about reading books and studying languages and engaging in arcane conversations reserved only for those with specialized training.

The word "theology" is a good place to start. The term itself includes two aspects: the idea of the *Logos*, which indicates that theology is a *logia*, a logic or language, and the subject matter of that *logos*—namely, *theos* or "God."

Theology can be the study of any number of gods; but Christian theology is about knowing the true and living God as he reveals himself through his *Logos*, his Word, Jesus Christ.

Since knowing God through his Word is the definition of being a Christian, we can see that all Christians are therefore Christian theologians. We are Christian theologians simply because we are Christians. It is therefore a complete misunderstanding of what theology is when you hear someone cheerfully (and perhaps also a bit scornfully) affirm: "I am not a theologian!" All too often what that will mean is simply that he or she is simply a bad theologian, failing to test everything in the fire of God's truth.

The question to ask any Christian is not "Are you a theologian?" We already know that he or she is. The question is whether the person is a good theologian or a bad theologian. We don't mean whether the person can remember the Chalcedonian definition or parse a Greek verb. Being a good theologian is not primarily about intellectual ability or about a list of academic credentials. Christian theology is, as Anselm famously put it, faith seeking understanding, and therefore *the* qualification for being a good theologian is faith in Jesus Christ, the revealing Word.

To be a good theologian is to seek to know and rely upon the Word of God better. It is to be a faithful Christian.

Yet, most of us don't go around introducing ourselves as theologians. In fact, whenever the topic of theology comes up (*if* it does), we are more likely to face the question "is theology even relevant?" Is theology out of touch with the day-to-day?

Theology is as relevant as every single choice that we make throughout the day. Each of us acts on the basis of our take on reality—which is to say that each of us lives theologically. There is nothing that is not a theological issue.

As Christians, we know that all our perceptions will be wrong if they are not shaped and informed by God's revelation. Christian theology is therefore the true "re-search," for it is about searching the whole of reality afresh in the light of what God has revealed.

To learn Christian theology is to clear out the junk that has accumulated in our minds through years of listening to the world around us, and to replace it with truth. It is to put on the mind of Christ and so sift out the lies in our culture that otherwise would drive us. It is refusing to drift with the assumptions of our society.

For example, much of today's culture is embedded in pragmatism. We want to be doing things. We feel that we don't need to think very hard about how and why and what we go about doing; we should just get on with it.

But what are the unquestioned (and unquestionably *theological*) presuppositions that shape this mentality? Is our activity good? Is our activity rightly directed? For instance, as Christians, we are eager to do evangelism. But what evangel should we share? The only suitable way to answer this question is through theological study, through wrestling with the Bible and the great doctrines that Christians have found there.

The only way for real change to happen in our lives and in the world is for theology to unearth and replace our presuppositions and assumptions about reality. That is how we get to turn the world upside down (Acts 17:6). Theology, therefore, simply could not be more relevant to day-to-day living. In fact, given that knowing God is a life-or-death issue, theology must have a life-or-death significance. If we see theology as irrelevant, we are calling God a liar by saying that his Word does not describe reality.

Theology is not a subject like other subjects, then. Rather, because of the universal claims of Christ, it seeks to boldly go where no mere discipline would dare, and inform every other branch of knowledge. The university grew out of the theological faculty, and, if the gospel is to be believed, may never leave it. As Abraham Kuyper said, "There is not a square inch in the whole domain of our human existence over which Christ, who is Sovereign over all, does not cry, 'Mine!'" Thus, in every aspect of our living and knowing, we should seek to be informed by the Word which is truth and not to be led astray by any other words that falsely claim authoritative knowledge.

As for us, it is theology—good or bad, Christian or pagan, thought-through or assumed—that will inform our approach to everything. So, do we believe in a coming judgment? Our answer to that can be seen in the extent to which we warn people of it. Do we believe in a monadic God, or in the personal God who is the Father, Son and Spirit? Our answer to that will determine whether or not we will ever genuinely be interested in relationships.

In particular, theology will inform our discipleship and evangelism. First, our discipleship: To use a remarkable expression of Paul's, theology is our "reasonable"[1] worship to God, and must involve our bodies: "I appeal to you therefore, brothers, by the mercies of God, to present your bodies as a living sacrifice, holy and acceptable to God, which is your spiritual worship" (Rom. 12:1). Our bodies (the way we actually live day by day) will either be used by us "in view

---

[1] Cf. Romans 12:1 KJV, which translates this phrase as "reasonable service."

of God's mercy" (cf. Rom. 12:1 NIV) or in view of something that is not the gospel. It is the job of theology to get a good view of God's mercy to ensure the former.

Good theology allows for good discipleship; bad theology must yield bad discipleship. A theology that does not involve bodily (real, active) service of Christ will not be a theology of *God's* Word, for if a theology remains merely "academic" in the sense of being "head in the clouds," then it cannot be a true theology of the Word who became flesh.

Second, theology will inform our evangelism, for to know this Word truly is to copy him, and so seek to go to the world and change it with his offer of salvation. Yet we are not only motivated by good theology to do evangelism. We are also equipped to do it. This is why Peter commands: "In your hearts honor Christ the Lord as holy, always being prepared to make a defense to anyone who asks you for a reason for the hope that is in you" (1 Pet. 3:15). In fact, it is often when you get out of the study to tell your friends about Jesus that you find you need to get back in there so that you can answer them better. Good theology of the gospel means a purer presentation of the gospel to a world that so desperately needs precisely that.

This, then, is why we should seek to improve our theology, because, for good or bad, the theology we actually have will inform all our discipleship, the enthusiasm and effectiveness of our evangelism, and our whole lives.

Does this mean that everyone should study theology professionally? That everyone should engage in the academic side of theology? And what about those of us who have done this—what should we be aware of as we embark on this path?

Everyone is a theologian, but not everyone has been given the opportunity to devote a large amount of concentrated time to this task of "re-searching" reality. Put so simply, it should be a joy to take our minds off our daily delusions and to fix them on the truth, which is good news.

However, as we know all too well, it is not quite that simple. At times we feel what a privilege we have been given in the opportunity to delve deeper into theology; yet studying for a degree in theology is not all quiet times and Bible study. Particularly when we are having to come to grips with some obscure point of grammar or when we are compelled to spend our time researching some musty corner of church history, it is easy to feel imprisoned in academic irrelevance.

So, what should we make of this kind of very practical concern in studying theology? How do make sure we are being good theologians at the desk and in the library?

The first encouraging thing to realize is that not everything that is alien or uncomfortable is bad. The problem with us evangelicals is that we can be like the fussy child that doesn't dare try any new food, simply because he doesn't know what it tastes like. We come to study theology with so many warnings in our ears about the dark powers of this occult subject—theology—and about how so many nice young Christians have been pulled down into the pits of liberalism through it. We start our courses and find ourselves bombarded with new ideas and new things to do, and so our suspicions seem to be confirmed.

We will see in a moment that there are indeed dark powers to be highly wary of in studying theology. But before that, we need to know that it is of the essence of theology to be shocking, disturbing, and confrontational.

The Word first confronts us as an offensive message about our sin and need of salvation. It disturbs us from the grave of our sin and replaces all the idols we have so comfortably relied on before sending us out to confront and disturb the world yet again. In fact, because of the confrontational nature of good theology, we might say that if you are not being disturbed and challenged by what you study, then you are not currently doing real theology.

There are no tourists in real theology. Theology should be a struggle as our world is turned upside down in the light of the gospel and as we are sent out by Christ to turn the whole world upside down. So, we should not automatically dismiss a strange practice or something we find to be unsettling and which challenges how we've been taught and how we think. For the true test of a good theology is not our level of comfort with it, but Scripture.

A case in point is the amount of time we are called upon to spend looking at what certain theologians have thought, rather than at the Bible. Isn't this strange practice somewhat a waste of time? Isn't learning about what humans have said a poor substitute for words that are divine?

Certainly, studying works of theology must never squeeze out Bible study, which must always remain as the immovable foundation of all our learning. And yet this alien practice is actually essential, for the God who is a community calls us to function in community. And so, one Christian will never have all the answers. We need to listen to and learn from one another.

We do theology as the church together, benefitting from the written wisdom of our fathers and mothers in the faith as well as our living brothers and sisters. This means that as we examine some theologian, however great or mistaken, we remind ourselves of our constant need for Christian fellowship. The lonely theologian is not the Christian theologian, who will love the community of the church. We study the Bible best when we are assisted by great and faithful Christians of the past as well as those Christians around and nearby us.

In sum, we do good theology in our studies when we struggle with the Word as it confronts us and the world, testing all things by it and not our personal whim, and when we do our study within the fellowship of the church, both past and present, learning from the wise and passing on their wisdom.

There is, however, another and more sinister reason why we should struggle as we do our theological studies. That is the presence of error and false teaching. In any other subject, error will have only limited repercussions that can often be simply blushed at or laughed at. In theology, the repercussions will be eternal. For in theology, error and false teaching distort reality itself, and can thus, as Irenaeus put it, be homicidal.

How should we be prepared to face errant theology? It is tempting, of course, simply to run away. And certainly, there are some theologies we will just have to leave for the moment, since on our own we are incapable of facing and dealing with them. This is yet another reminder of the need for fellowship as well as the fact that just because we are individually incapable of answering some problem does not mean the church as a whole is.

However, error and false teaching are not going to go away before Christ returns. And so we must prepare ourselves and the wider church to tackle these spiritually murderous ideas. Part of the point of studying theology is to be equipped to do just that. We have thus been placed in an immensely responsible role within the church—as we know Christ more, we are better equipped to tackle all that is opposed to him and his gospel. And seeing that, we find that, for whatever reason we enrolled on our course, we have now been saddled with a duty that forbids us to be lazy in our studies. For the health of the church and the world, we must confront error and false teaching with the saving truth of the Word of God.

To do that, we must realize that we go into the fray with "the sword of the Spirit, which is the word of God" (Eph. 6:17). In fact, before we even think about stepping out like that, we need to be sure of our own spiritual diet. Before swallowing any theology, new or old, we must ensure it is edible and nutritious by passing it through the proving fire of Scripture. As Paul puts it so many times: "Test everything" (1 Thess. 5:21); "[Do not go] beyond what is written" (1 Cor. 4:6); "Let God be true, and every man a liar" (Rom. 3:4 KJV). When we do this, actively rejecting what Scripture proves to be false and (full of prayer and praise) embracing what we find to be true, then studying theology will no longer be a time of spiritual stagnation or backsliding, but of wonderful growth. For, in times when the church has been forced to counter heresy, God has so often brought us to even clearer understandings of his truth—witness the early Christological debates and the Reformation, for example. And in all of our seeking after truth, we get to know more of God's greatness and graciousness.

We have seen that we are to reject the false teaching and error *around* us. But there is another danger for the student of theology, and that is that the theology can turn ugly *inside* us.

The easiest and most common way for that to happen is for us to allow theology to become theoretical and speculative. Just as we can become anaesthetized to both love and violence on TV, so theology (and worst of all, the Bible) can become a mere subject for us to study coolly.

Rather than theology being our worshipful response to God's revelation, we can use it to make absurd godlets of ourselves as we proudly flaunt our so-called "knowledge" in front of our bewildered "non-theological" brothers and sisters in Christ. This is not real knowledge, because it is based on the fundamental error of thinking that truth consists of data rather than a Person (John 14:6).

This kind of study leads us in the wrong direction. It is so easy to catch yourself, as you're reading your Bible, and find that you're not learning of Christ, but simply wondering what Wellhausen would say, or making mental notes to use the verse in the next essay. It's a short step away from our actual task of helping the church to do theology and towards making theology a specialist science that no "mere Christian" can do. The horrific end result is that, instead of having grown in our knowledge of Christ and so matured in faith, we have become a pharisaical intellectual priesthood, preventing God's good news from spreading through the world. We have become, then, enemies of the gospel.

So, as students of theology—which we should always remain—we must daily ask ourselves if our theology involves real, bodily service of the Word and life in the church. Or, more simply, do we do theology to know Christ better, or do we use it to hide ourselves, like Adam, from his gaze?

We have seen that to do Christian theology is the greatest thing possible for a human, because it is not simply about lectures and books, but about knowing

Christ—"re-searching" reality and re-tuning our lives in the light of his revealed truth. We can also see that, so far from being irrelevant, it is the most logical thing in the world to know this *Logos*, to make him known, and to seek to replace all other competing words with him.

Then our studies yield eternal fruit. It is only when we fall back from actively seeking to know him, and so let another word determine our lives, that we become illogical. Thus, our studies should only lure us to know him more and to entice others to live in reality by enjoying this true queen of the sciences.

9

Run the Race

On May 13, 1940, Winston Churchill gave his first speech to the House of Commons as Prime Minister. Famously, he told them: "I would say to the House as I said to those who have joined this government: I have nothing to offer but blood, toil, tears, and sweat. We have before us an ordeal of the most grievous kind. We have before us many, many long months of struggle and of suffering."

Jesus is able to say something quite different to his people: he promises victory. Jesus offers life and joy and peace. But enlisting in the army of Christ and entering into a life of gospel ministry does mean struggle. It does mean suffering. There are casualties. It does mean blood, toil, tears, and sweat.

Today and every day, the church sends out troops into the battlefield. And whenever we do so, I feel such a fierce surge of pride on behalf of those whose love for Christ has led them to give their lives for his Name. When I think of those who are called to shepherd the flock, I have both a dream and a nightmare. The prospect that terrifies me is that some of them could become what Jude calls "shepherds feeding themselves," "fruitless trees," "wandering stars" (vv. 12–13).

And the dream—the ambition that burns and drives my own ministry—is that one day, these servants of the church may be able to say with Paul, "I have fought the good fight, I have finished the race, I have kept the faith" (2 Tim. 4:7–8). That one day, they will see the eternal fruit of their labor and that Christ will crown them with glory and say, "Well done, good and faithful servant!" (see Matt. 25:23).

Friends, Hebrews talks of the race set before us (12:1). It's a race set before all Christians, but it's so appropriate for those embarking on gospel ministry. Shepherds, you have a war, a race set before you. And you are called not to fidget, not to slouch, not to meander, but to run. It is the greatest and most thrilling race of all. It is the race of following Jesus.

Earlier, in Hebrews 6, Jesus is spoken of as our fore-runner (v. 20). He is the pioneer, running the path of death and glory. He is the advance guard, clearing the way. Through suffering, through humiliation, through death—he is carving a sure way for us through it all to glory. He is the horn of our salvation, going ahead, powerfully subduing our enemies.

That, friends, is the race you are called to. Going where he has gone—all the way. This means that today we are not just saying "well done" to those who are heading out into the fields of harvest. The church sends out martyrs—witnesses—men and women who are called to die. Men and women who are therefore called to a glory that those who will not die to themselves will never see.

And that is a beautiful and thrilling thing. Perhaps someone hearing these words has never experienced the joy of deep repentance, the bittersweet thrill of letting go your own pride and ambition, of finding yourself born again to a bigger, brighter vision—where great Christ, not little self, fills your gaze.

It doesn't make sense to the self-obsessed, but this is the happiest, most liberating race you can run. And our little passage gives us three comforts for runners: look back to the martyrs, look up to Jesus, and look forward to joy.

First, look back to the martyrs. "Therefore, since we are surrounded by so great a cloud of witnesses" (or martyrs), "let us also lay aside every weight, and sin which clings so closely, and let us run with endurance the race that is set before us." Look to the cloud of witnesses whom the Lord has already helped finish the race.

One of the greatest dangers of leadership is isolation. People don't understand the pressures that are on you. Perhaps they elevate you and don't think you need encouragement. Perhaps they don't dare advise, so they throw rocks from a distance. Leadership just has that tendency to isolate you. So, you need to fight the isolation.

Two friendships that I formed in college—that is, the friends I still meet up with three times a year—are so important because we are able to support and encourage each other with complete honesty and genuine love. And I'd urge you to establish that kind of support group around yourself. If you don't have friends that close, work to develop them. Stick together.

Earlier in Hebrews we were told, "Let us consider how to stir up one another to love and good works, not neglecting to meet together, as is the habit of some, but encouraging one another, and all the more as you see the Day drawing near" (10:24–25). And here in chapter 12, the call is not to run in isolation. No, it's "let us run with endurance the race that is set before us."

But even when you *are* all alone—shattered on a Sunday night, having preached yourself out, your heart full of all the pastoral difficulties on your plate—there's always the cloud of witnesses. You can always return to the exhibits of the hall

RUN THE RACE 111

of faith in Hebrews 11. There's a lesson for every situation there. There are brave and faithful saints who have been kept through adversity. And there are foolish failures, just like us. There's Noah the drunk: the Lord helped him finish. There's David the adulterer: the Lord helped him finish.

Even in moments of discouragement—in fact, particularly then—make time to read church history. Read Christian biographies. Time and again, you'll see that you're not alone in your struggles, your weakness, your ups and your downs. There's a cloud of witnesses all testifying how the Lord brought them through. So, look back to the martyrs.

Second, look up to Jesus. "Let us run with endurance the race that is set before us, looking to Jesus, the founder and perfecter of our faith." And that is the heart of how to run. You run the race *by looking to Jesus.* That's where new life began for you. "Look to Me, and be saved, All you ends of the earth," says the Lord (Isa. 45:22 NKJV). And you looked to the Son of Man lifted up, and you lived (cf. John 3:14).

Keep doing it. As Hebrews 12:3 puts it, "Consider him." It is the sight of him that brings life, and courage, and perseverance, and humility, and grace for the needy. Even if you forget everything else from your studies, remember this: "Consider him." It's as simple an order as a king can give. "Consider him."

How easily you could laugh, thinking "don't you know the theological wisdom I've amassed? Don't patronize me." But so strong is the gravitational pull, even in gospel ministry, away from Christ. Spiritual coldness, professionalism, preaching that ticks a box but doesn't even seek to move hearts, discouragement because your eyes are fixed on the successes of others, pride because your eyes are fixed on the successes of your own ministry, fear of others, despair—all these are the fallout of not fixing your eyes on Jesus. And all these are cured, ultimately, with those simple words: "Consider him."

Therein lies integrity. Therein lies spiritual freshness and power. And that's exactly what you see in Hebrews 11, in the great cloud of witnesses. The saints there prove that faith, that strength to run the race, is not some inner resource you have. It does not come from stiffening the sinews and summoning up the blood. It always comes through looking to him.

Why, for example, did Moses choose to be mistreated with the people of God than to enjoy the fleeting pleasures of sin? Hebrews 11:26 tells us: "He considered the reproach

RUN THE RACE 🏃 113

of Christ greater wealth than the treasures of Egypt, for he was looking to the reward." Like Moses, "consider him."

Look back to the martyrs, look up to Jesus, and finally: look forward to joy. This really is just part of looking to Jesus. Run, Hebrews 12:2 urges, "looking to Jesus, the founder and perfecter of our faith, who for the joy that was set before him endured the cross, despising the shame, and is seated at the right hand of the throne of God."

It was the joy set before him that enabled Jesus to endure the cross and despise the shame. And what was that joy? It was not just the thought that his Father would raise him to life again. It was not just that he would ascend to the throne of heaven and rule. He'd had all that. He never had to leave home to enjoy that.

No, it was the fruit of all he had accomplished: the bride he had come and bled to redeem. It was the prospect of hearing "the voice of a great multitude, like the roar of many waters and like the sound of mighty peals of thunder, crying out...

> 'Let us rejoice and exult
>   and give him the glory,
> for the marriage of the Lamb has come,
>   and his Bride has made herself ready.'" (Rev. 19:6–7)

The joy set before him was the marriage: his union with his Bride. The joy set before us is the same: to be with him, face to face, all sin and pain removed. Like him, we will see the fruit of our labors: we will see those the Lord has given us, redeemed. These helpless sinners, now brothers and sisters, will be all around us at the wedding feast.

Friends, think on that prospect, and compare it to the competing joys you set before yourself. Do it right now: think about that private, deeply cherished dream you have for the future. To be married? To be popular? Influential? To be comfortable?

It may not be that that dream is a bad thing in itself. But whenever you think of it, hold it next to the great joy set before you. And think: which is the more compelling? Which is greater? Which is the more sustaining joy, the joy to set front and center before yourself?

Brothers and sisters, don't settle for a lesser race, a race towards a fickle and uncertain hope. Success, money, fame, comfort will all eventually disappoint you. Run the great race of death and glory.

Go with the cloud of witnesses. Go after our great forerunner. Go towards joy.

About the Author

Michael Reeves is President and Professor of Theology at Union School of Theology, where he teaches in the areas of systematic and historical theology and also on preaching and spiritual formation. He is a local church minister, Senior Fellow of Newton House in Oxford, Director of the European Theologians Network, and speaks and teaches regularly worldwide. He is the author of several books, including *Rejoicing in Christ, Delighting in the Trinity: An Introduction to the Christian Faith,* and *Rejoice and Tremble: The Surprising Good News of the Fear of the Lord.*

Union

We fuel reformation in churches and lives.

Union Publishing invests in the next generation of leaders with theology that gives them a taste for a deeper knowledge of God. From books to our free online content, we are committed to producing excellent resources that will refresh, transform, and grow believers and their churches.

We want people everywhere to know, love, and enjoy God, so glorifying him. For this reason, we've collected hundreds of articles, podcasts, book chapters, and video content for our free platform. We also produce new streams of written, audio, and video resources to help you to be more fully alive in the truth, goodness, and beauty of Jesus.

If you are hungry for reformational resources that will help you delight in God and grow in Christ, we'd love you to visit us at **unionpublishing.org**

Reformation Fellowship

Reformation Fellowship is a global movement of
pastors, ministers, students, missionaries and believers
who share a common vision: to see reformation in
Christ's church worldwide.

Through publications, theological input, biblical
resources, podcasts, webinars, and every other means
at our disposal, we desire to create a culture of gospel
integrity and gather a global movement of believers
under the gospel banner of Christ.

Join the fellowship:
reffellowship.org

Union

Be prepared for a lifetime of ministry and mission with a degree from Union

---

FOR GROWING LEADERS AND MINISTRY TRAINEES

GDip: Taught through local Learning Communities, the GDip offers robust theological training to equip you for fruitful ministry.

BA (Hons):   This course provides you with a theological, practical and spiritual foundation for a lifetime of serving Christ's church.

FOR CHURCH LEADERS

MTh: With full and part-time options, the MTh provides a feasible way for church leaders to study alongside their existing ministry commitments.

---

*Discover more and apply today at **ust.ac.uk***

Also Available

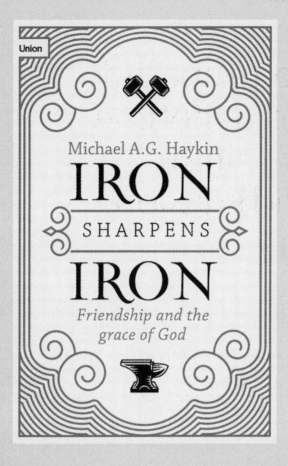

With its emphasis on speed and busyness and the mis-named "social" media, the modern world has not been an especially welcoming place to develop long-lasting, solid friendships that nurture the heart. Providing exemplars and guidance in this challenging situation, this book on friendship looks at some of the details of the friendships of the eighteenth-century pastor-theologians Andrew Fuller and John Ryland to help us think about and engage in meaningful relationships that provide joy and strength for the Christian journey.